WHERE IS GOD?

Where Is God?

Christian Faith
in the Time of Great Uncertainty

JULIÁN CARRÓN

in conversation with
ANDREA TORNIELLI

translated by Sheila Beatty

McGill-Queen's University Press
Montreal & Kingston • London • Chicago

© McGill-Queen's University Press 2020

Originally published in Italian by Piemme, an imprint of Mondadori,
as *DOV'È DIO? La fede Cristiana al tempo della grande incertezza:
Una conversazione con Andrea Tornielli*, by Julián Carrón.
© 2017 Edizioni Piemme; © 2018 Mondadori Libri S.p.A.

ISBN 978-0-2280-0096-9 (cloth)
ISBN 978-0-2280-0198-0 (paper)
ISBN 978-0-2280-0195-9 (ePDF)
ISBN 978-0-2280-0196-6 (ePUB)

Legal deposit first quarter 2020
Bibliothèque nationale du Québec

Printed in Canada on acid-free paper that is 100% ancient forest free
(100% post-consumer recycled), processed chlorine free

Funded by the Financé par le
Government gouvernement
of Canada du Canada

Canada

Canada Council Conseil des arts
for the Arts du Canada

We acknowledge the support of the Canada Council for the Arts.

Nous remercions le Conseil des arts du Canada de son soutien.

Library and Archives Canada Cataloguing in Publication

Title: Where is God? : Christian faith in the time of great uncertainty / Julián
    Carrón in conversation with Andrea Tornielli ; translated by Sheila Beatty.
Other titles: Dov'è Dio? English
Names: Carrón Pérez, Julián, interviewee. | Tornielli, Andrea, 1964– interviewer.
Description: Translation of: Dov'è Dio? : la fede cristiana al tempo della grande
    incertezza. | Includes bibliographical references and index.
Identifiers: Canadiana (print) 20190206225 | Canadiana (ebook) 20190206268 |
    ISBN 9780228000969 (cloth) | ISBN 9780228001980 (paper) | ISBN 9780228001959
    (ePDF) | ISBN 9780228001966 (ePUB)
Subjects: LCSH: Christianity—21st century.
Classification: LCC BR121.3 .C37 2020 | DDC 230—dc23

This book was typeset by True to Type in 11/14 Sabon

Contents

Preface

Four Days of Questions with No Internet

Is it still possible to meet God in our times, in this liquid society that surrounds us? Do the secularization and de-Christianization characteristic of a formerly Christian West signal the end of times or just the end of one time and the beginning of another? Should we battle a plural and relativistic society by raising barriers and walls, fortifying mountaintop citadels to repel attacks, or accept the opportunity to announce the Gospel in a new way? Do the end of Christian civilization and the difficulty of finding common denominators in values and natural morality mean that sincere dialogue between believers and non-believers is impossible? Or do the times demand new forms of dialogue? Why does Pope Francis, following the lead of his predecessors in the last half century, insist so much on mercy? Are there preconditions we must meet to encounter Christ on our road as those who crossed paths with Him 2,000 years ago in the villages of Galilee did? Is the encounter with Him the fruit of marketing strategies, the outcome of a method put into practice, like following an instruction manual, or is it a gift of pure grace and as such not ours to possess, neither before nor after the encounter? Is the Church a society of perfect people who spend their time judging everything and everyone, perhaps with daily invectives against modern times and nostalgia for the past? Or is it made up of Christians who consider themselves poor sinners, wretches who through grace have been pardoned, who need forgiveness and mercy every day, who at times reflect the gaze of mercy onto others near and far, never considering themselves better or more virtuous?

In a situation that in some respects increasingly resembles early Christianity, how are those who believe in Jesus called to live? Fr Julián Carrón has led the Communion and Liberation (CL) movement for fourteen years. His none-too-easy task has been to take up the baton from Fr Luigi Giussani, who, though he did not intend to found anything but simply to repropose the essential elements of Christianity and belonging in the Church, gave life to a structured movement. Like all new realities, that movement has evoked and still evokes controversy. It has been and continues to be the object of discussion.

I was interested in talking with this Spanish priest born among the cherry orchards of Estremadura, to whom Giussani, at the end of his life, and to the surprise of many, entrusted the leadership of the movement. This conversation did not focus so much on thorny internal issues in the life of CL and the Church more generally – though this book does cover those issues, with questions and answers that are sometimes uncomfortable – but primarily on how the movement views the historical moment we are living in. It lets us hear, with minimal self-referential terminology directed at insiders who are already loyal customers, about the essential core of the Christian faith, with particular attention to the dynamic by which Christianity has been and still is communicated.

This book is the fruit of four days of dialogue that took place in the big meeting room on the top floor of the Sacred Heart Institute in Milan, from which we could see the eastbound bypass and feel the floor shake slightly every time a truck hurtled by. The meeting room seemed like any other, without any particular distinction to its furnishings. Only on the last day did Fr Julián tell me that this room was where Fr Giussani, who needed assistance because he had Parkinson's disease, spent his last days and died.

In the dialogue with Carrón, we looked not so much at the beginning of the movement as at the beginning of Christianity, the Gospel stories, because the rediscovery of its origins, plumbed and lived today, answers the question about how believers in Christ can bear witness in our time.

In response to those who seem to need an enemy to rail against daily in the name of Christian values, to those who seem to exist exclusively to oppose and contradict, Fr Giussani's August 1982 comment on the Action française of Charles Maurras – who in the early twentieth century wanted to reshape the world in the name of Christian values – seems more apt than ever. "But it was not faith," Giussani said. "Faith is only this: ... the vigorous openness to a presence," to the presence of Christ.

> The fundamental objection to the continual recovery [of such an awareness] derives ... from an existential insecurity, that is, from a deep fear that causes you to seek grounding in your own expressions, [in your own achievements:] culture and organization ... It is an existential insecurity, a deep-seated fear that causes you to perceive the things that you do culturally or organizationally as your own grounding, as the reason for your being. Thus all the cultural activity and all the organizational activity do not become the expression of a new physiognomy, of a new person. If they were the expression of a new person, they could even not exist, when circumstances did not permit them, but that person would remain standing. Instead, if there were not these things, many of our people here today would not be able to stand, would not know what they are here for, would not know what they adhere to: they would not be; they would not have substance.[1]

One could add: if they did not have enemies and fellow believers to rail against daily, they would no longer know who they were or the source of their substance.

In *The Christian Adventure*, Emmanuel Mounier predicted, "The doorkeeper of history will not listen to your arguments: he will look at your faces."[2] And even before the doorkeeper of history, the people we meet every day look at the faces of Christians more than they listen to their lessons of doctrine, perceiving the human fondness and sincere compassion of those who embrace without judging because they themselves were and are continually embraced and forgiven.

The dialogue that the reader will find in these pages is not about the history of CL (there are already such books), nor is it a biography of Fr Julián Carrón (whom I thank for having accepted my proposal and for never refusing to answer any questions), or even a book on the movement. Rather, it represents the attempt – the success of which will be up to the reader to judge – to ask and evoke questions, to discover or rediscover the substance and dynamics of Christianity, to inquire whether and how these substance and dynamics can be interesting and testified to anew in a society that is not yet post-Christian but well on the way to becoming so.

Andrea Tornielli

WHERE IS GOD?

I

Encountering God Today

When Secularization Becomes an Opportunity

Fr Julián, we live in a world racked by wars, terrorism, hunger, and migrations. How does a Christian look at the future with a panorama like today's?

A Christian looks at the future with realism and hope, two terms that seem almost contradictory. In fact, for some, nurturing hope means having a rose-tinted outlook on reality, while for others, being realistic necessarily means having no hope. Instead, hope is precisely what enables an authentic and radical realism that has no need to erase any part of what exists, in one sense or the other. For this reason, the only realistic gaze is the Christian one. Saint Paul offered perhaps the most apocalyptic description of his contemporary world in the beginning of the Letter to the Romans, not because he was a fiercer observer than others, but because the hope created in him by the encounter with the risen Christ enabled him not to step back from the facts and problems, but to realize what was wrong around him. He did not need to see reality with rose-tinted glasses.

We see today the same attitude in Pope Francis, who speaks with great realism about the situation we are experiencing, with a piecemeal Third World War, arms trafficking, violence, "throwaway" human beings, the phenomena of migration, injustice, hunger, and corruption. Equally interested in the particular vicissitudes of individuals and global scenarios, he has become a world leader everyone acknowledges precisely because his gaze is full of the realism born of Christian hope. If a Christian truly lives an experience of faith, the certainty that it brings extends to the future; that is, it grounds a hope that enables you to face everything with a new gaze.

Are you saying that Christians are not pessimists, but neither are they optimists?

Fundamentally, in the final analysis, they are optimists, not out of naiveté, but because the final word on life and reality is the event of Christ, a fact that happened and that introduced into history an otherwise impossible hope. A line by Charles Péguy expresses this well: "To hope … you would have to … have obtained, received a great grace."[1]

What does "a great grace" mean? Can you explain briefly?

It is the grace of the encounter with Christ, like the encounter – very human – of the first two, Andrew and John, with Jesus on the banks of the Jordan River, that changed their entire lives, or Saint Paul's shattering encounter on the road to Damascus, that totally overturned the outlook he had had until that moment. The encounter with the living Christ determined their way of looking at everything and opened them to grasp the irreducible positivity of reality. The ultimate point that defines reality is no longer evil and suffering, but the victory of the risen Christ. Those who receive the grace of the encounter with Christ – the gratuitous, unmerited gift that does not depend on how good we are – and welcome it, begin living with His presence in their eyes, in every fibre of their being, and it shapes the way they look at reality.

The very word conversion draws upon this looking at everything with another gaze, from another perspective.

Yes, the Greek word *metanoia* (conversion) means the change of the *nous*, the mind, the way of conceiving, because of the introduction of a new, unforeseen factor – a presence – that is the source of a new consciousness.

What does Christian faith have to say to the men and women of today, in a world so fragmented and problematic, in a society defined as liquid, in which certain self-evident principles recognized

by everyone have disappeared? Your book Disarming Beauty
*begins with the question of whether a new beginning for faith is
possible today, now that the foundational convictions Christianity
created have collapsed.*

I am convinced that faith can say and give a great deal to
women and men today, if they encounter it incarnate in life in
the experience of other people. In fact, the life faith generates
is attractive: how many people, having encountered it, do not
want to lose it! Unfortunately, it is not rare for many of our
contemporaries to come into contact with a faith reduced to
mere moral precepts or memorized formulas. I am thinking
of how much the Kantian version of an ethical Christianity
has affected our mentality, or how some identify Christianity
as a list of abstract doctrines, without seeing the advantageousness for life. When this happens, people remain un-
touched and see no connection between faith and life. Instead, when they meet Christians whose lived faith enables
them to face the circumstances everyone faces – difficulties,
tiredness, disappointments, illness – in a different way, with
greater human intensity and an ultimate gladness, then everything changes, and they are amazed, struck, and intrigued.
Out of this impact arises an attraction, a curiosity that can
become an explicit question about the origin of what they see.
This is the Christianity that happens anew, that needs no pre-
requisite to capture a person's attention. Just seeing how a certain person goes to work provokes an unexpected curiosity:
"How is it that at eight in the morning you always come into
the operating room singing?" I am talking about a specific
case with a first name and last name. If a person who arrives
at work burdened sees another who faces the same circumstance in a totally different and more human way, it is natural
for that person to ask, "How is this? What happened to you?"
When we run up against another way of living daily life –
which, to use the words of Cesare Pavese, "is the life that crip-
ples a man"[2] – we can realize that faith concerns life in its concrete nature and in its entirety.

As we see in history, Christianity succeeded in transforming reality not when a king who converted and was baptised forced his subjects to do the same but when it was communicated bit by bit, as by osmosis, from person to person, from family to family, above all through women, mothers.

In the first centuries, Christianity had perhaps its greatest moment of expansion through merchants, slaves, and mothers of families, very normal people who simply by living the everyday life of everyone, as we read in the Letter to Diognetus, documented the difference I just mentioned. It was not due to any effort of theirs, or ability, not because of any acquired merit or intellectual superiority, not because they had something special, not because they were perfect. No, they had limits like everyone else, but they had had an encounter that transformed them.

This is what Emmanuel Carrère said in his book *The Kingdom* regarding the reaction the first Christians evoked. "At first, they understood the reason ... And then, people start to understand. They start to see the interest, that is, how much joy, how much strength, how much intensity life gained from that apparently senseless conduct. And so they had only one desire, to do as the Christians do."[3]

Probably they testified to a capacity to love one other, a capacity to share, just as we read in the Acts of the Apostles.

This is precisely the point. I often told the kids at the school in Madrid where I taught for years, "Christ should interest you precisely so that the most beautiful things in life can last." Falling in love is one of these. But often the impetus of when you fall in love does not last over time. Who can make it last? Loving the person you so desired, loving her truly, without bending her to yourself, to your own demands, turns out to be an impossible undertaking. And what happens with love happens in the rest of life, in work, in relationships with people, in everything. There is a lack of duration that we cannot solve. What enables the most beautiful experiences of life to last? We have to acknowledge that all our efforts and attempts are insufficient. There is a line by T.S. Eliot that I like very much: "Where is the Life we have lost in living?"4 In fact, you often have the sensation of losing life in living, as if something that begins in a fresh, attractive way inevitably becomes routine over time, wears down, and loses its fascination. Something other than us, greater than us is needed. For the human person, this is Christ present.

So then, what does it mean to live the Christian experience in a context like that of Western society, marked by secularization?

I would say first of all, as I have observed before, that the context of secularization in which we are immersed paradoxically makes it easier to grasp and live the substance of Christian experience. In fact, where Christianity is lived this way, precisely because of the contrast, you can perceive more clearly the human intensity, the "extra" capacity for affection, for freedom, for facing even adverse circumstances with hope, for using reason in a way that is not reduced, that is born of the Christian event. Ideals and ideologies have fallen short, values and self-evident principles that united us for centuries have collapsed, but the human heart continues to desire. Therefore, secularization can turn out to provide us Christians with a great opportunity for testimony.

How would you define the phenomenon of secularization? What does it mean to live in a secularized context?

Secularization is a very complex phenomenon whose effects we all observe: much of what Christianity contributed to building has disappeared. In order to understand this, you must go back to the threshold of modernity. In the societies of the time, the Christian faith permeated and determined much, if not everything. Then Christian unity ruptured and the Protestant Reformation created the conditions for the so-called religious wars. If people no longer shared a common religion, what was left to bind them together? Reason. The title of Kant's well-known work *Religion within the Boundaries of Mere Reason* gives you an idea (*a posteriori*) of what direction he took. In a famous talk in Subiaco, then-Cardinal Ratzinger explained very succinctly the intuition of the Enlightenment. "In the age of the Enlightenment ... in the situation of confessional antagonism ... they tried to keep the

essential moral values outside the controversies and to identify an evidential quality in these values that would make them
independent of the many divisions and uncertainties of the
various philosophies and religious confessions. The intention
was to guarantee the bases of life in society and, in more general terms, the bases of humanity. At that time, this seemed
possible, since the great fundamental convictions created by
Christianity were largely resistant to attack and seemed undeniable."[5] The shared acknowledgment of these values made it
possible to overcome the divisions and controversies arising
from the clash of confessions, while separating the values
from the confessions.

Thus they tried to separate the values from their origin?

Yes, the Enlightenment attempted in a certain sense to preserve the fruit of the previous historical experience, but free of
bonds with the particular and concrete history in which they
arose. It is very interesting in this regard to read a line of Kant's
that clarifies this point: "In fact, one may quite easily believe
that if the Gospel had not taught the universal ethical laws in
their whole purity first, reason would not have known them in
their fullness."[6] Therefore Kant acknowledged that the Gospel
is the origin of certain values. But he added, "Still, *once we are
in possession of them*, we can convince anyone of their correct-
ness and validity using reason alone."[7] This is the crucial point.
By then, the essential values made known by the Gospel could
be autonomous as self-evident principles. There was no need
for anything other than reason in order to recognize them,
so undeniable did they seem. However, this Enlightenment
attempt – no different than every other human attempt – has
had to deal with history.

What has happened from the age of the Enlightenment to
our times? Have these great convictions withstood the
changes of history? As he concluded his description of this tra-
jectory, Ratzinger said, "The search for this kind of reassuring
certainty, something that could go unchallenged despite all
the disagreements, has not succeeded."[8] Those values are no
longer shared and acknowledged by all as they were previous-

ly. This is what I call the collapse of the self-evident. Just think of the value of the person, which restrictions of various kinds (such as on freedom of expression and of association, the right to publicly profess your faith, protection of work and the family, etc.) are limiting in many Western countries and which is entirely denied in many parts of the world. Or the value of solidarity, rejected with the building of new walls, after we tasted the joy of finally seeing the fall of the Berlin Wall. And again, who would have thought that the value of life would be lost, or that democracy would be questioned? Just a few decades ago this would have seemed like an exaggeration, while now it is clear to everyone: certain fundamental values have disappeared.

In this regard, I witnessed something I will never forget, because it speaks more eloquently than a thousand rational arguments. Years ago during a trip to Uganda, I met some women of Kampala who were all AIDS victims. A nurse friend of mine had moved heaven and earth to provide them with medicine to ensure an acceptable quality of life, but after taking the pills once or twice, the women stopped, because they no longer knew why they should keep on living and therefore let themselves drift toward death. For them, even the evidence of the value of life was obscured.

I am amazed that some of the great Christian thinkers of the late 1940s and the 1950s had already perceived what was happening.

Whom do you have in mind?

I am thinking of Montini, de Lubac, Giussani, Guardini, and von Balthasar. Each of them, by different roads, perceived the signs of a collapse that began in a time when it seemed that everything still endured. For example, I am amazed by an expression of de Lubac's, which I recently reread (in *The Drama of Atheist Humanism*): the attempts of the Enlightenment thinkers, to put it concisely, "often preserved a number of values that were Christian in origin; but, having cut off these values from their source, they were powerless to maintain them in their full strength or even in their authentic integrity."[9] We are talking about reason, freedom, truth, brotherhood, justice, that is, those great things without which there is no true life or fulfilled humanity. Now, separated from their source, these great things "become … empty forms. Soon they are no more than a lifeless ideal," until they appear "unreal."[10] This is exactly what we are living today.

And therefore in this context, in this situation, what is needed?

For the empty forms to become life again. For the values to become real, carnal, concrete, and historical in our experience once again, as they did when that Ugandan nurse began looking at the women with AIDS with an interest in their persons that made them rediscover their worth and realize they were greater than their illness. From that moment, their desire to live was rekindled and they began taking their medicines again. The encounter with the gaze of that nurse restored flesh to a value that had become unreal, making it once again visible to their eyes and desirable.

The values of the person, of solidarity, and of freedom that we all care about defending make life more human. But the very fact that today certain issues are raised tells us that those values have been emptied, becoming unreal. This is the challenge we must face. What is happening? How can we face the situation without proposing "solutions" that have already proven to be a failure? Travelling around the world in these years, I have encountered many people willing to dialogue about this, because all of us share certain questions and concerns, and they affect everyone, from political parties to institutions, from citizens to cultural associations. It seems to me that the current situation offers a great opportunity to establish a relationship with people who have different origins and histories. In this context, Christianity can make a contribution, but only if we witness to its true nature and live it in its essential nature. This is what the pope has invited us to do on many occasions. When Christianity is proposed in its original form, as an event of life, as a fascinating and concrete presence of a new humanity, it can attract interest once again in a secularized society. A situation like the one we are living in demands that we discover our origin anew.

Therefore, do you think secularization can become an opportunity?
Yes, certainly.

But are you saying that you do not view the situation in which we find ourselves negatively?

No Christian can take joy in a situation like the one in which we find ourselves, one that threatens so many things that are beautiful and fundamental for our life. But it is good, as Guardini says, to expose the "dishonesty" of attributing certain values to a sort of "evolution of human nature" and progress of history, when instead they are actually linked to Christian revelation.[11] When this dishonesty "characteristic of the image of the modern era"[12] becomes clear to all, we will understand the newness and the contribution that Christianity brought to the emergence of fundamental values such as those of the person, freedom, work, and the possibility to live life with hope. The trustworthy reason for hope will be seen more clearly.

Put this way, doesn't it seem you are just interested in scoring points for Christianity?

No, I am not saying it in a one-sided way in support of Christianity but as an opportunity for understanding the contribution that Christianity offered in the past and can offer today for facing many of today's problems. Even secular historians acknowledge it, for example the great Le Goff, who said, "I am not a believer and do not practice the faith, but as a historian and medievalist I must acknowledge ... the role that Christianity played as a spiritual force and creator of values in determining the originality of Europe."[13] This brings to mind a recent paradox: for quite a while there has been controversy about and refusal to discuss the Christian roots of Europe, but a year ago, the same sphere where the discussion bogged down [the European Parliament in Strasbourg] decided to award Pope Francis the Charlemagne Prize! I am not saying that they did this to recognize the connection between certain values

and their Christian roots. I am only saying that when you
come upon a testimony like that of Pope Francis, Christianity
becomes real again, shows its capacity to help people face their
problems, and returns to being interesting even in the eyes of
the most unlikely people. This is just one example of what happens, and much more often than we believe. Many people
think they already know what Christianity is. They already
have their own judgment, or prejudice, grounding their decision that it no longer concerns them. But then, when they encounter people who, experiencing concrete problems and
challenges, testify to the human benefit that comes from a gaze
of faith, they begin to be interested in Christianity again. I
always tell my students that Christianity is communicated
through envy: seeing that the life of a Christian is fuller, more
intense, more capable of embracing difference and of loving
the other, kindles a desire to live this way.

Giovanni Battista Montini [later Pope Paul VI] arrived as arch-
bishop in Milan in the mid-1950s and realized something that was
not as evident in Rome in the same period. The image of the Church
was still that of a strong, structured entity able to move the masses
– just think of the great gatherings around Pope Pius XII. Instead,
in Milan the signs of secularization were clearer. Fr Lorenzo Milani
also recognized this phenomenon in a dramatic way. Secularization
did not happen after the [Second Vatican] Council, as some ideo-
logues affirm.

Archbishop Montini realized in Milan that there were worlds
that had become impervious to the Christian faith, for example,
those of finance, fashion, and the factory workers in the periphery
of the city. It was not that they had become anti-Christian. The
Christian faith simply interested them less, or no longer interested
them. Montini's episcopate and papacy were an attempt to
respond to the question of how to announce the Gospel to people
today. I was always struck by Paul VI's gaze upon the reality of the
world. In an editorial published in Azione Fucina *in 1929, thus*
many years before, Fr Battista Montini had written that the Chris-
tian does not look at the world as an "abyss of perdition" but as "a
field ripe for the harvest."[14] The world remains the world, as

described in the Book of Revelation. What changes is the positive gaze of the Christian.

In these decades we have seen an acceleration of what Montini perceived in the 1950s, when the situation appeared solid, Catholic associations still had many members, and everything seemed to indicate that after the two world wars there would be a religious rebirth. Only the most acute spirits began to see that something was not right, that something was broken, that the transmission of the faith as lived experience was interrupted. Now everyone can see it. The process we have seen in recent years is the widely confirmed revelation of what some began to perceive many decades ago. Montini was early to recognize the emptying and shifting underway in society and in Christian people. But, as you observed, what is very interesting for us is his attitude toward the difficulties and contradictions he saw emerging: a gaze full of compassion, tenderness, fondness. For this reason, I have said it before and I will say it again, the situation we are living now is an authentic opportunity to regain awareness of the nature of Christianity. In fact, faced with secularization, an attitude of intransigence can arise, an absolutely negative gaze, that sees the world as "an abyss of perdition," to use the words of Montini's editorial. Instead, one can see the world as "a field ripe for the harvest," with the gaze Paul VI and the [Vatican] Council showed us.

Deep down, the Church has never lost that positive attitude, and certain great contemporary Christian figures have incarnated this clarity of judgment, this original fondness for human reality. I think of Péguy, in that famous passage of *Véronique* describing the position of Jesus facing the world. In fact, there is a deep analogy between the era of the Roman Empire and ours. Jesus came and did not spend the three years of His public life whining over or cursing the wickedness of the times. "He cut short. Oh, in a very simple way. Creating Christianity," said Péguy.[15] This is exactly what Pope Francis is doing today, and his predecessors before him, in the relationship with a world that is in turmoil, that is searching for a mooring, a gaze full of mercy that enables people to carry on with the journey and not be destroyed by their mistakes. Today, as Christians, we have the opportunity to rediscover and live anew the modality with which Jesus looked upon the world. How many times in the Gospel do we discover it: "At the sight of the crowds, His heart was moved with pity for them, because they were troubled and abandoned, like sheep without a shepherd"?[16] This gaze of mercy contains everything that Christ introduced into the world.

But how can we rediscover and communicate that? Primarily by experiencing it ourselves, coming up against someone through whom the gaze that Jesus turned to the crowds or to Zacchaeus reaches us. To the degree to which we accept it, we begin to look at ourselves and the world as Jesus does. Pope Francis shows us this in every action he takes. We know full well that this is not something we can take for granted, because at times a Christian can have a very rigid attitude.

The Greek verb that describes Jesus's compassion speaks to us of a visceral love, of a compassion that is born in the deep instinctual maternal and paternal heart of parents when they see their little newborn. God is deeply moved in this way when looking at women and men.

To my mind, this tells us everything about why the Mystery became flesh, became a man. God became flesh so that we could experience and "see" His mercy, His infinite love for us, His moved emotion in the face of our nothingness. When the Invisible became visible through the birth of Jesus – a baby, who then grew, who walked the roads of Galilee – we were able to see One who was deeply moved by the pain of a widowed mother at the funeral of her only son at Nain. That woman felt herself looked at in a way that has no equal. Jesus, with a tenderness without compare, in a way that is inconceivable for us, told her, "Woman, don't cry!" and then He restored her living son to her, but first He told her, in a rush of emotion, "Don't cry!" Or think of the tenderness that Jesus felt for Mary Magdalene in tears in front of the empty tomb, when He said to her, "Mary!" Everything she had experienced with Him on so many occasions seemed insufficient in the face of the drama of His death. And so Mary Magdalene, as she cried, as she looked around at everything that sur-

rounded her, starting from that weeping, from that wound provoked by the death of Christ, felt her hope awaken at that
"Mary!" This is God with us. As Pope Francis said recently, "Try
to imagine, right now, with the baggage of disappointments and
failures that each of us carries in our heart, that there is a God
close to us who calls us by name and says to us, 'Rise, stop weeping, for I have come to free you!'"[17]

Through the happening of this gaze of love and mercy,
Christ makes Himself present and makes it possible for us to
experience Him now. He does not refer us to a memory of the
past, written in the Gospels, but is a "present presence." Therefore, I would like to say that what the women and men of our
times need is not so much the verbal repetition of the Christian announcement, but to encounter people changed by
Christ, in whom that gaze is flesh. As I said, this holds first of
all for Christians. In fact, this is the gaze Christians discover
upon themselves, as a desirable and unexpected gift. By the
power of this gaze we can look at any circumstance, any mistake, any pain, with hope.

Actually, Saint Augustine said, "In manibus nostris sunt codi-
ces, in oculis nostris facta."[18] *That is, we have in our hands the
Bible, the Scriptures, the story of the Gospels that speak to us of Jesus.
But before our eyes we have "facts," that is, real and contemporary
testimonies.*

For years, I was a Biblicist and teacher, and I must say that
this is the only way to introduce us to the Gospel in a way that
is not reductive. I remember a girl who had met a group in her
parish, in a city near Madrid. She had grown up without any
Christian education. But through a series of encounters, she
began spending time with this group of people, going to eat
with them, taking part in their initiatives, and at a certain
point she also began going to Mass with them. Listening to the
Gospel the first times, she commented, "The same thing that is
happening to me happened to the people in the Gospel!" In
listening, she could not help but begin with the present, precisely as Saint Augustine said, "The volumes are in our hands,
the facts before our eyes."

When I taught religion in school and began explaining the Gospels in order to talk about Jesus, the students told me, "What's written in the Gospel is very beautiful, but it doesn't happen anymore." This is the great challenge that concerns the very nature of Christianity. During the Enlightenment, Lessing said that if he had lived at the time of Christ and seen the miracles He did and the fulfillment of the prophesies about Him, Lessing, too, would have believed; and if he saw them happen in the present through the work of some Christians, certainly Christianity would be interesting for him.[19] Setting aside Lessing's personal opinion, the statement captures the problem: many people have not had the opportunity to encounter a lived Christianity, which is the only one that can awaken the interest of a real person. This is a problem that concerns us, and its gravity echoes in a memorable line of Eliot's: "Has the Church failed mankind, or has mankind failed the Church?"[20]

We can complain about secularization, but we should also ask ourselves what responsibility we Christians have for this situation, through the way we have lived and live our faith. Many people have left Christianity deliberately, while others have broken away almost without knowing it, but I wonder – without wanting to measure anyone – how many have distanced themselves because they have not seen a faith incarnated in daily reality, in true and living testimonies, full of humanity? As we observed before, in order to make Himself known to us, God wanted to make Himself visible, otherwise He would have remained an unknown mystery, a stranger, and we would have continued to perceive Him far away, to the point of feeling He was unreal. Through the Incarnation, entering into history as a man, the Mystery conquered us, awakening in us an attraction without compare ("*delectatio victrix*," Augustine called it),[21] first of all in the shepherds and then in those who were witnesses to His humanity, actions, words, and miracles. Today as well, I repeat, this is the only way Christianity can evoke interest, by touching the needs of people.

There is another characteristic that Christians and non-Christians share, I think. We read in the Gospel that those who follow Jesus are people who do not feel "in the right," publicans and sinners who have questions about life and their lives, humble people who allow themselves to be wounded by reality. The same thing can happen today, through a passage from the Gospel, an encounter, or something that happens. Letting ourselves be wounded means we allow ourselves to be challenged, and realize we do not know everything. It means we have not already judged everything, and that we are not always in the teacher's chair. It seems to me that often this attitude is missing among certain Christians, too.

There is a beautiful passage in the Gospel in this regard, directed at those who put themselves in the teacher's chair and do not let themselves be wounded by reality because "they already know." "To what shall I compare this generation? It is like children who sit in marketplaces and call to one another, 'We played the flute for you, but you did not dance. We sang a dirge but you did not mourn.' For John [the Baptist] came neither eating nor drinking, and they said, 'He is possessed by a demon.' The Son of Man came eating and drinking and they said, 'Look, he is a glutton and a drunkard, a friend of tax collectors and sinners.'"[22] This passage expresses well what you just said in your question. People can always harden their hearts, close in on themselves, not allow themselves to be touched by reality, whether it be through the sound of a flute or through Jesus. It seems impossible, but it happens. They decide to reject it, decide to say no. "I will not allow this reality to wound me. I want to get rid of it." Anyone can have this attitude, Christians included, anyone who thinks, like the scholars of the law and the Pharisees, that they already know everything. This is the position that Jesus reproves the most in the Gospel. It is very interesting to see how He reacts when faced with such presumptuous close-mindedness. He provokes the people in all sorts of ways, trying to open a breach in them, forcing them to think, "According to you, is it lawful to heal on the Sabbath?" The Pharisees held their tongues because they were worried about the reaction of the people who were there waiting for Him to heal the sick. So then Jesus did the miracle, but He did not settle for just this. He pressed those who thought they knew everything with a question that silenced them: "Who among you, if your son or ox falls into a cistern, would not immediately pull him out on the Sabbath day?"[23] He nailed them with an example from daily life, to make it evident to everyone how reasonable it was to behave in the same way with the sick who asked to be healed on the Sabbath.

Jesus did not allow Himself to be trapped in a legalistic attitude; He allowed Himself to be struck by the wounds of the people and showed another way of conceiving of things: the Sabbath was made for man, not man for the Sabbath. This is the newness that He came to bring. His gaze introduced an absolutely new way of relating to people, to their fragility and their need. "Those who are well do not need a physician, but the sick do. I did not come to call the righteous but sinners."[24] He did not come for the healthy, the just, those who already knew, but for the sick, the sinners, those who suffered from their weakness and helplessness. It is crucial for each of us: the day we are no longer aware of our infirmity and wretchedness, we will no longer realize the grace of having Someone who can heal our wounds. We will no longer need Christ.

I am very struck that Jesus Himself is moved and challenged by the reality He encounters, with mercy that is divine and compassion that is human. He lets Himself be questioned by reality. That first miracle at the Feast of Cana was not in His plans. He did it because His mother asked Him to. There is something unsaid in that Gospel story: why did Jesus change His mind after having reacted negatively to the request? His mother must have looked at Him as only a mother can look at a son, making Him understand that He really had to do that thing. Similarly, Jesus was deeply moved by the widow of Nain and also by the crowd that seemed like sheep without a shepherd. Therefore, this letting yourself be wounded is first of all a characteristic of Jesus. If Christians do not continually allow themselves to be wounded by the reality they encounter, they cannot announce the Gospel, because the Gospel is announced if you man-

age to communicate it, if you enable the other to perceive that both
of you are in the same boat, that you are not better than the other.
It is simply that you have received a grace, rather than a disgrace,
but you are never one who judges, who prejudges, who condemns.
You are someone who participates in the same humanity, the same
wound. The pope always strikes me because when he goes to prisons,
the first thing he thinks and says is, "It could be me in that cell, if
the circumstances of my life had been different." The Gospel is
announced by communicating that we are part of one humanity
and that we all need someone to heal us and at the same time keep
this wound open.

What you say is part of the challenge that today's world con-
fronts us with. But the Gospel, as we have just seen, and the testimony of the pope help us to face the present time and show
us the adequate point of departure. First of all, let's be attentive
to our experience: we are the first to have needed someone to
help us be struck by our wounds. We often forget that if Christ
had not bent over, and does not bend over our weakness
through the embrace of the people He has used and uses, we
would be unable to look at ourselves. The more we yield to His
presence and forgiveness, the more we are moved to embrace
others and let ourselves be struck by their wounds. The problem arises because we often think that this embrace is something sentimental, that is, that the mysterious gaze of Jesus
does not contain a judgment about what the human person
truly is. But let's consider the woman at the well, or Zacchaeus.
Who truly grasps deep down what I am? Who can truly reach
all the humanity of the other? Those who see the five husbands
or those who also see the deep thirst of that woman? Those
who only see the sins of the publican Zacchaeus, or those who
also see the anticipation that made him climb a tree to see that
man he had heard about?

With His gaze, Jesus does not yield to sentimentalism but
introduces a new judgment that does not reduce people to
what they are capable of doing, to their potential for performance. In all His mysterious nature, Jesus sees the thirst for
fullness even when it is buried under a heap of sins. The

Samaritan woman had had five husbands, and the man she was living with was not her husband, but Jesus did not start with that. He began by asking her for water to drink and then spoke to her about the living water that she could not help but desire, that is, the happiness she had sought in vain in all those relationships that were unable to quench her thirst. Deep down, everything we do, including many of our sins, is an attempt to respond to the thirst that constitutes us: we look for the answer in the things that cannot give it to us, and for this reason we always have to start over in search of what satisfies us. In the end, you become skeptical and do not believe there can be an adequate answer to your expectation.

Jesus introduces a different gaze on the human person and reveals that we have a structural relationship with something Other; He shows us that the thirst is something we are comprised of. Jesus did not accept the moralistic reduction of the human person to performance. From then on, the Church has always in some way had to deal with the temptation to reduce Christianity to a sort of moralism that measures people on the basis of their capacity for consistency. But consistency is a grace: it comes from the encounter with He who fulfills me, who is more me than I am, and without whom I would not be myself.

So then, is this the only thing that frees us from evil?

The encounter with He who fulfills us is the only way to be freed deep down, at the root, from the impulse to possess people and things that characterizes us. On their own, people cannot free themselves and end up seeking an answer to their desire for fullness by possessing things and people. In her simplicity, that Samaritan woman understood well the alternative that Christ set before her and that He introduces into everyone's life: "If you do not accept the water that I give you, you will continue to be thirsty for the rest of your life."

Jesus responds to the needs of the human person. After He multiplied the bread and fish, everyone felt exuberant. They recognized His exceptionality and wanted to make Him king, but He slipped away. The next day He was in Capernaum and the crowd returned, looking for Him. Seeing them, Jesus was moved, and truly loving all those people, He told them, "Look, the bread that satisfied you yesterday is not enough to satisfy your hunger and your thirst. I am the bread of life; whoever comes to Me will never hunger, and whoever believes in Me will never thirst. Nothing else can fill your life."[25] Jesus is not only the answer to human limitations and sinfulness, but He is also the answer to the thirst for fullness – or in other words, the desire for happiness – that is the nature of the I. If this desire is not answered, it is not possible to get to the heart of the human problem; it is not possible to face the question of evil. This is why Jesus's gaze on the human person is so powerful: "What profit is there if you gain the whole world, but then lose yourself? What use is it to obtain everything you want, if you then lose yourself, that is, if what you obtain cannot fill your life and you do not find something that truly satisfies it?"[26]

I have often told the story of a conversation I had with an Italian girl who lived in Barcelona. Among other things, she painted, and as you know, the dream of a painter is to succeed in having a big show. Finally she managed to organize it, and it was resoundingly successful, far beyond her expectations. But then… "After the big success, I spent the whole afternoon crying," she told me. Why in the world? It was not enough. So then, what is enough? This is what the great figures have discovered, sooner or later. For example, the day Cesare Pavese received the Strega Prize, he said to himself, "In Rome, apotheosis! And so?"[27] The dramatic nature of life and the insatiability of desire emerge from the depths of success, not of failure. The content of the Christian announcement is that the answer to this thirst for fullness in each of our hearts has become a man, Jesus, who died and rose and is present today in history. But it is necessary that His presence reach me today, in the experience of a concrete and real encounter. Otherwise, like everyone else I will be a prisoner of some image of an answer, grasping onto some good that will cry out to me, "Farewell!" – as Rebora says in his poem. [28] The one way to be free from the tyranny of possessions and projects, and thus from evil, is to have such a powerful experience of living, an experience of such great fullness, that there is no longer any need to grab as many things as you can, or to bind people to yourself, in order to feel alive.

If this does not happen, it is unlikely that in a situation like the one in which we live, where nobody cares about calls to ethics, something in the concrete life of individuals can truly change.

One thing really struck me about the example of the Samaritan woman. It is true that in speaking to her, Jesus tells the truth about her life and therefore asks her about the husbands she has had and about the man with whom she is living, who is not her husband. But that dialogue provides a beautiful indication about the method for entering into contact with people. The first words that God address-es to this woman are not a statement, not a list of her sins, not a con-demnation or judgment. Jesus's first words to the Samaritan woman are a question. God asks her for some water to drink. "Give me a drink" is the way He enters into contact, into dialogue with her. He does not emphasize her sins and mistakes but asks for something.

God looks at us with the same trepidation as a mother observing her newborn, entirely defined by the desire for hap-piness that sooner or later will emerge in that child. As the years go by, that child will make many mistakes, but the moth-er's gaze will remain the initial one. Jesus looks at the human person in the same way, not reducing man according to his limits but considering the infinite desire that cries out from within those limits. He made us in order to fulfill that desire. But why did God make us? What need did He have to create human beings? It was out of an explosion of the love that lives in the core of the Trinity; He wanted to share His own being, His own fullness, with someone. He could only do so by gen-erating a creature with infinite desire. Saint Augustine expressed this in a very beautiful line: "Thou has made us for Thyself, and our hearts are restless till they rest in Thee."[29] Peo-ple in the Middle Ages spoke about *desiderium naturae*, to say that the human person is defined by this desire inscribed in the heart.

If God made us with this desire, we wonder how, or in what, it can find an answer, since everything in reality is limited. The things we come up against have the nature of a sign; everything bears a message that says, "Further on!"[30], as Montale said: everything points beyond. It is as if everything was telling us, "It is not I. I am only a reminder."[31] Reality appears like a reminder of another reality, of a face toward which we are led. If a person does not find this face or does not remain open to this "other reality" or systematically rejects it, her life empties, flattens, or collapses into desperate restlessness that can also burst into violence. I am thinking of the phenomenon of terrorism in its current version. As I said after the attacks on the Bataclan club in Paris, so many young people arrive here in Europe, or are born and grow up in our cities, and find emptiness instead of an answer to their desire or an education to search for it; they breathe a kind of nihilism, often explicit, but more often implicit, that is the condition from which violence and desperation can arise in many people. Now, this is our great responsibility: we who by grace have encountered an answer, the "beyond" made flesh, who continues to be present in history through the human companionship of the Church, have been called to testify to Him with our life. We have been given a grace to share, so that others can touch it with their hand and know that an adequate response exists to the thirst of their heart.

In a society like ours, so smashed as it is, what can attract anew the heart of the human person?

The human heart is drawn only by encounters with people who, through grace, experience a fullness of life that others can touch through the way they face reality, deal with circumstances, and live relationships with a heretofore unknown freedom. This is the power of Christianity: content and method coincide in it. Its truth reveals itself in a phenomenon of changed humanity, in a life event, in "facts," in a transformed human reality in which you see concretely that existence can be complete and lived in fullness. Only this can interest those who are aware of their thirst for destiny, who realize that their own desire for happiness finds no satisfying answer anywhere. Above all today, in a context in which the dearest value is one's own freedom, and nobody allows anything to be imposed on them, only an attraction can move them. It is no coincidence that Pope Francis continues to quote a beautiful expression of Benedict XVI's, "The Church does not engage in proselytism. Instead, it grows *by 'attraction.'*"[32] This is what Jesus did: He turned to our freedom, attracting it, and to our desire, corresponding to it. He came into the world in a society – first-century Judaism – that was much more varied than the societies of following centuries. As we know from the Gospel and from Jewish literature, this society was full of different groups: Pharisees, Zealots, Sadducees, and Essenes, to name a few. In the Roman Empire, as well, Christianity found itself faced with a pantheon populated by every type of divinity.

Christianity has never had a problem with living in a multicultural society. Rather, it revels in it, because all the diversity and originality of the Christian proposal can emerge in this context, without impositions on anyone. The Second Ecumenical Vatican Council gave us back the awareness that the only way to communicate the truth is through freedom. In fact, the truth needs nothing more than its own beauty to reach the heart of the human person. This is why I entitled the book that came out two years ago *Disarming Beauty*. In a multicultural and multi-ethic world like ours, in which certain evidences and shared values no longer hold, Christianity can interest people only through the attraction it evokes and nothing else.

I am always struck by some things that the Gospel emphasizes, the examples, the stories, the parts introducing the narration of what Jesus said or did; for example, when the evangelists tell us how great crowds of sinners and publicans hurried to gather around Jesus. These people did not feel righteous; they were "irregular," borderline, judged harshly by the society of the time. They were not "respectable," but they had a question about their own lives and for various reasons were considered marginal. They had a question and Jesus attracted them like honey draws bees. They were in search of something and followed Him. In contrast, those who already knew all the doctrine, who believed they already knew everything and considered themselves righteous, looked at Jesus really negatively. I believe that this is also a judgment on our times, on the current situation of our Christian communities, and on the way we live our faith. If a Christian community follows Jesus, it should attract sinners, not shun them.

That is exactly right. The important thing is to grasp, within an experience, the gaze Jesus turned on the people He met. At times, we ourselves do not think that a person truly desires much more than what she or he can possess. Often, those on the borderlines, those who do not settle for a bourgeois life, sense the need for something more, for travelling roads that may be extreme or contradictory, as we see today – and as happened for the Samaritan woman – to seek satisfaction for their thirst for fullness. Even though Jesus said He did not want to change one comma of the Mosaic law, these people who were searching, suffering, and struggling nonetheless saw that He had a different gaze on their need and weakness, a gaze that they found nowhere else, quite different from what they had experienced with those who judged and looked down on them, who believed themselves already justified and saved. In Jesus we find at one and the same time a fierce defence of the Law ("not the smallest letter or the smallest part of a letter will pass from the law"[33]) and also a gaze that welcomes, forgives, and regenerates, enabling people to journey to reach the ideal. The two elements are not contradictory. Rather, starting from this gaze that forgives and realizes the expectations of the heart, the law can truly be fulfilled.

Following the attraction of His person, through their experience of fullness, they realized that they no longer needed to sin, to err, to treat themselves badly, to allow hate to prevail, or to take advantage of others in order to affirm themselves. In this way, they realized how essential the relationship with Jesus was to keep them from succumbing to evil. Now, when we forget this, we invert the terms of the question and reject people who are difficult or disoriented, or in other words, those who have many wounds. Instead, Jesus asks us to welcome them and rebuild the humanity, to be "restorers of ruined dwellings," as Isaiah said,[34] to regenerate the fabric of society.

This reminds me of the gaze of which the pope spoke in his letter Misericordia et misera, *published at the end of the Jubilee [2016]. Francis wrote: "Here what is central is not the law or legal justice, but the love of God, which is capable of looking into the heart of each person and seeing the deepest desire hidden there; God's love must take primacy over all else. This Gospel account, however, is not an encounter of sin and judgment in the abstract, but of a sinner and her Saviour. Jesus looked that woman in the eye and read in her heart a desire to be understood, forgiven and set free. The misery of sin was clothed with the mercy of love. Jesus's only judgment is one filled with mercy and compassion for the condition of this sinner."[35] Jesus's gaze is for that woman in particular. He read her heart. First there is the embrace of love; before everything else, there is a God who loves you.*

What the pope says is truly crucial. In the Gospel episode of the banquet where Jesus is a guest, when the notoriously sinful woman arrives, the Pharisee thinks that Jesus is a bit naive, or worse, simple-minded. "Don't you understand who this woman is? You shouldn't bless her!" Instead, Jesus challenges his judgment and tells him the parable of the two debtors. "'Two people were in debt to a certain creditor; one owed five hundred days' wages and the other owed fifty. Since they were unable to repay the debt, he forgave it for both. Which of them will love him more?' Simon said in reply, 'The one, I suppose, whose larger debt was forgiven.' He said to him, 'You have judged rightly.'"[36] So He makes the Pharisee understand that He is not as naive or simple-minded as he assumes. Jesus knows full well who that woman is, and precisely because He knows, He forgives her, untying the knot of pharisaical logic. With His action, He shows that the one way to solve the problem of that woman is to look at her with love. Only this would bring about a change. Jesus is anything but a sentimentalist who is clueless to reality or pretends not to see it. He sees it very well, in fact much more deeply, and knows the origin of that woman's sins.

Recently I heard the story of a Brazilian prisoner who had escaped from many prisons in his country. At a certain point, he was sent to one of those prisons where there are neither officers nor weapons, the APAC (Amando o Próximo Amarás a Cristo), an experience begun a few decades before by a group of Christian volunteers led by the lawyer Mario Ottoboni. After a few months, the judge who had sent him there went to see how things had turned out for that prisoner. He saw the man was still there in that prison from which he could have escaped easily. "Why haven't you escaped from here?" he asked. "Because here I am loved, and you don't run away from love." None of the rules, regulations, and legal instruments are sufficient to overcome evil. This love defeats evil. Without it, all the attempts will always fail. Who can awaken this love in people? Only the one who has the truly realistic gaze on the human person, a gaze that is called mercy, limitless forgiveness. Jesus is the mercy that fills and penetrates history, present now through the human instruments He uses, as demonstrated by the experience of the APACs, among many.

2

The Millstone of Evil versus Mercy

When Natural Law Is No Longer Evident

Fr Julián, why is it so difficult to believe today?

Because we are distant from ourselves. Who is interested in Jesus? Those who need Him. And who needs Him? Those who are aware of their own wounds, their own sickness, their own evil, their own dissatisfaction, their own sinfulness. Those who feel they are missing something and perceive the drama of their own incompleteness need him, those whom life has put to the test, those who have experienced that even achieving their greatest objectives does not give them the fulfillment they had hoped for. These are the people who have understood Jesus's importance for their lives and have followed Him. Becoming aware of your own incompleteness makes it possible to open yourself to something else: "What am I looking for?" You have to go deep into yourself. What can awaken our thirst when it has been weakened, or in many ways distorted, and reduced? Being looked at gratuitously, without conditions, without measure, or in other words, encountering someone who has the same gaze as Jesus.

Everyone who goes through difficulties, trials, and contradictions – those at the borderline, the irregulars – and lives through any dramatic situation needs to be looked at the way Jesus looked at, embraced, and loved people. But, mind you, their answer does not occur through our design. It is not the outcome of a mechanism, like when we put a coin in a vending machine and a drink comes out. The possibility of their "yes" does not depend on us, but on God's design and their freedom. As Christians, we have the task of testifying that there is an answer to people's wounds and needs, no matter what their condition.

This point is interesting and also liberating. It is not a mechanism, not the outcome of a marketing strategy or a project, and there is nothing taken for granted, also because, as we see in our daily experience, sometimes becoming aware of your lack of fulfillment can lead to an even greater desperation, an even greater close-mindedness. The trials of life can close off any little glimpse of light. At times, in order to be able to survive, you think you have to forget the incompleteness and the wound it causes. Maybe you pretend they no longer exist, burying them under a thick layer of ashes or making them bearable with a heavy dose of anesthetic.

This is the alternative to the Christian proposal: to convince yourself deep down that in order to live better you have to eliminate the wound and the incompleteness, do away with the desire, or reduce it. Often those who find no answer try to park their desire someplace, to silence or bury it. Today we see many people who are running away from their own "I," who do not want to stay with themselves, in order to avoid dealing with their own structural incompleteness. "All this is small and insignificant compared to the capacity of one's own mind," to use Leopardi's expression.[1]

Before Christ, people tried to reduce desire. It was dangerous to desire; it was hubris. Disproportionate desire could lead to madness. In the Greek world, the rule was thus to attenuate desire, to impose a measure on it. This is understandable, because only if you are in front of an adequate answer can you liberate all your longing; otherwise it is better to limit it, to avoid being destroyed by continual disappointments. Only Jesus can look at people without diminishing them, because He knows their mystery deeply and has a proposal that responds adequately to their desire. This is why the only reasonable gaze on the human person is that brought by faith. Thus it is not surprising that today there is a return to fearing desire and reducing it. I am reminded of a scene in Ingmar

Bergman's film, *Fanny and Alexander* (1982). At a certain point when the family is at table, there is an emblematic dialogue. "We Ekdahls have not come into the world to see through it. We are not equipped for such excursions. We might just as well ignore the big things. We must live in the little, the little world. We shall be content with that." What does life become, then? "Take pleasure in the little world. Good food ... gentle smiles ... fruit trees in blossom, waltzes."

Two thousand years after Christ, we are returning to the Classical world. Far from the Presence that takes all our desire seriously, we are unable to look at ourselves and life in its entirety; we must settle, recognizing that we are not equipped to face the big issues alone. People need to encounter a presence that measures up to the greatness of their desires, so that they will not yield to either form of reduction.

Think of the parable of the prodigal son. He had everything, a house, a father who loved him, the belongings he needed, but none of this was enough and he felt constricted. Many people have abandoned a comfortable situation in their families because they were unsatisfied, at times reducing themselves to doing the strangest things. The prodigal son felt his heart pulsing with the urgent need for something more and tried to imagine what could meet that need. He lived the way he wanted, and in the end realized that none of those things he had imagined were enough to satisfy his desire. Thus, disgraced, alone and needy, "he came to his senses" the Gospel tells us, or in other words, he regained the awareness of his own needs and felt the desire to return home, not out of moralism, but because he discovered that the only place he could truly be saved and fulfilled was in a relationship.[2] "I shall get up and go to my father and say to him, 'Father, I have sinned against heaven and against you. I no longer deserve to be called your son; treat me as you would treat one of your hired workers.'"[3] What made him return? The recognition that the answer to his desire was in that relationship, the true value of which he had initially failed to understand. With this parable, Jesus explains to us what saves our desire, freeing it from the images we force it into: the relationship with He who has made us. Outside of this relationship, we will always be like wanderers without a destination, in search of something that satisfies us, and sooner or later we will end up in boredom, as Moravia said, because boredom is the recognition that everything is insufficient.[4]

Another way of anesthetizing it is to dismiss it as an experience of adolescence, a transitory moment of life that coincides with youth and then is covered by life and the cynicism that accompanies it.

But during the vicissitudes of life, in certain painful or traumatic moments, or when we realize that things we invested ourselves in turn out to be disappointments, the desire reemerges. It is not in our power to impede it.

What are the reasons for believing in the existence of a superior Being who created us, who loved and continues to love us?

This is a demanding question, and I think it relates with what we have just said. To some, wondering about the existence of a superior Being may seem irrational or only for specialists, extraneous to those who have vital and concrete interests, something for those who have nothing better to do, or at best, for the rare philosopher who still addresses certain problems. Now, as long as we live on a superficial level, in forgetfulness or banality, we can more or less get by and avoid the question. But when life presses, when there is provocation from something that happens, a situation, a lack of fulfillment, a failure, a restlessness we do not know how to solve, then certain questions explode and burn in us: "Why is there suffering, pain, and death?" "What meaning does life have?" Those questions we censured and sought to elude begin to reemerge. The religious problem coincides precisely with these questions.

When events happen like the collapse of the hotel in Rigopiano, or the tsunami of a few years ago, or the Germanwings airplane crash in the Alps, even newspapers feel obliged to give space to certain questions, precisely those that contemporary culture tries to quiet, as if it were shameful to talk about them. As Rilke said, "And all combines to suppress us /

partly as shame / perhaps, and partly as inexpressible hope."[5]
At times like these, we see headlines such as "Only silence,"
"Facing the void," "Why are we human beings?" and "What are
we?" We thought we could live without asking ourselves certain questions; we thought we could censure them, but the
reality of our constitutive needs erupts from within our experience when we least expect it. In this way, we find ourselves
once again dealing with what we had tried to set aside. Life is
this continual provocation. We try to stop up the flow of certain questions in all sorts of ways. We try hard to distract ourselves, but reality continues to knock on our door and forces
us to deal with it. Unless we perform or undergo a systematic
reduction of what happens to us, we cannot avoid questions
about the meaning of life and the reality around us. These, not
others, are the religious questions.

But you did not answer my question …

I am getting there. What is the point of departure? Reality,
which knocks on the door of our experience and makes all our
need for meaning emerge. When I was a religion teacher, a
young man in the lunch line at school asked me, "But are you
sure of what you say about God?" I answered, "Yes, because, you
see, what distinguishes my position is that I do not start out
from God: I start out from reality." In fact, reality, with its presence, is what asks us the question. How? In order to help us
understand this, Fr Giussani, in one of his best-known works,
The Religious Sense, invited us to imagine this situation. If I were
born now and opened my eyes for the first time, but with the
awareness I have in this moment at my actual age, what would
my first reaction to reality be? I would be dominated by wonder at the presence of things, a presence that I do not make,
that I find, that imposes itself on me.[6] You could object that
this is only imaginary, but I would say no, it is the original
experience of our relationship with reality and it would be easy
to recognize it if we were not normally prey to the obvious. A
young man who had been in a coma for several months told
me that when he woke up he looked at all of reality with

absolute wonder. It was no longer something obvious, but a "given," the presence of which made him grateful and inspired him to question his assumptions.

Along these lines, often when I teach at the Università Cattolica in Milan I talk about reality as a sign and give an example. "Imagine when you get home that you find a beautiful vase of flowers in your room. What would your first reaction be?" "Wonder." "And right after?" "Who sent them to me?" I ask, "And why are you sure that there is a someone?" "Only because of the presence of the flowers." It is impossible not to be provoked by reality. Certainly, there is always the possibility of a partial or unsatisfactory response. Continuing with the same example, let's imagine that a girl finds the flowers in her room and goes to her mother and asks, "Who brought them for me?" And her mother answers, "Why do you ask who brought them to you? They're there because they're there." The girl would not be satisfied with this answer. There might be someone in her position who would decide to settle: "They're there because they're there; I'll enjoy them until they wilt, and then it's over." But it is clear that the answer does not correspond to the question that the presence of reality provoked. The girl, pursuing the provocation represented by the presence of the flowers, will insist on looking for an adequate answer, because the best thing about the flowers is not the flowers, which she can enjoy until they wilt; the best thing about the flowers is that they refer to the person who gave them to her. She is interested in discovering who loves her so much that he sent them to her. Now, what happens with the flowers happens to a much greater degree with all of reality, with the life of each person.

So then, what makes people capable of acknowledging a superior Being? The provocation that reality represents for our reason, for our freedom. Neither common people nor scientists, in the degree to which they are open to it, can settle for partial explanations that do not satisfy reason's need for totality.

There have been great scientists who did not agree with this reduction of reason. Albert Einstein wrote to Maurice Solovine,

You find it strange that I consider the comprehensibility of the world (to the extent that we are authorized to speak of such a comprehensibility) as a miracle or as an eternal mystery. Well, a priori one should expect a chaotic world which cannot be grasped by the mind in any way. One could (yes, one should) expect the world to be subjected to law only to the extent that we order it through our intelligence. Ordering of this kind would be like the alphabetical ordering of the words of a language. By contrast, the kind of order created by Newton's theory of gravitation, for instance, is wholly different. Even if the axioms of the theory are proposed by man, the success of such a project presupposes a high degree of ordering of the objective world, and this could not be expected a priori. That is the "miracle" which is being constantly reinforced as our knowledge expands. There lies the weakness of positivists and professional atheists who are elated because they feel that they have not only successfully rid the world of gods but "bared the miracles." Oddly enough, we must be satisfied to acknowledge the "miracle" without there being any legitimate way for us to approach it. I am forced to add that just to keep you from thinking that – weakened by age – I have fallen prey to the parsons.[7]

And the greatest "miracle" is the existence of the "I." The cosmos reaches a point of evolution in which it gains awareness of itself; the "I" is the self-awareness of the cosmos. I was very struck by the words of an important Spanish scientist with whom I had a recent conversation. "With my scientific reason," he said, "there is something that I still cannot explain: the 'I' of my children," an "I" that is not attributable to the sum of their biological or historical antecedents. Here it is necessary to accept evidence that cannot be resolved by a calculating reason but requires an open reason in its essential intertwining with freedom. In *Apologia pro vita sua*, Newman wrote that when he was fifteen years old, walking along the road, he was thunderstruck by the intuition that there were "two and only two supreme and luminously self-evident beings: myself and my

Creator."[8] Giussani commented on this passage, highlighting that the intuition of the existence of God is the ultimate implication to which the existence of the "I" points. Accepting it is a decision of freedom and therefore always involves the experience of risk.

Once, during a lesson when I gave the example of the flowers, there was a girl who was not persuaded at all, and discussing it with her did not change her mind. It was the first time that she had come to lesson, invited by a friend. During the break between one hour and the next, one of the students present went out, I do not know where, to get a flower, which he then put at her place. When the lesson started again, the people near her were curious to see her reaction. I observed the scene from the teacher's desk. She betrayed no reaction, which seemed to confirm that what she had defended in the previous hour was her normal attitude. But I knew the friend who had invited her, and she later told me what had happened. "Then and there, she didn't react because since I was the only person she knew in the classroom, she assumed I had put the flower there. But when I assured her, swearing to it, that I was not the one, she began racking her brains to think of who could have done it. Even though she had asserted the opposite during the lesson, she spent the whole afternoon asking herself who had given her that gift."

Accepting the ultimate implication of the existence of the "I" – admitting that I am "You-who-make-me," Fr Giussani said, with reference to God, to the Mystery who makes all things – is perhaps the most dizzying decision of freedom and demands the use of reason in all its breadth. Something similar happens with love. We do not see love: we perceive its signs. There is no magnetic resonance machine able to detect love. The instruments of scientific inquiry cannot grasp it. At best they might be able to measure the increase of the activity of certain parts of the brain when we love or when we hate. But its presence is too evident to be denied: it imposes itself through signs. Just think for example of the love of your mother.

Perhaps one of the greatest difficulties today, even more than belief in God, in a superior Being, is about the existence of evil, about pain, especially pain suffered by the innocent.

For this reason, in many cultures there has been an effort to explain the great problem of evil with the dualism of two original principles, one good and the other evil, that reverberate in a good creation and an evil creation. The people of Israel challenged this concept, marking an absolute break from it. The first page of the Book of Genesis expresses their conviction about the good nature of reality: "And God saw that … it was good … it was very good."[9] Even though the surrounding cultural context was characterized by the co-presence of polytheism and dualism, the Jews did not affirm this approach. The origin of everything is goodness; the origin is good. Even though the people of Israel experienced evil, suffering, deportation, and slavery, this positive gaze on reality dominated. What makes this possible? A history. If the metaphysical dualism, the affirmation of the two principles of good and evil did not prevail, it was because of the experience the people of Israel had of God. Through their history – made up of victories, trials, greatness, the epic wandering through the desert for forty years – God revealed Himself to the people of Israel in His goodness, in His saving power. From this experience, the people of Israel concluded that He, the savior, is also the creator and that there is one good principle at the origin of everything: God. Since everything that exists comes from God, it is also equally good. Reality is positive, and evil is a lack of good, a distancing of oneself from the good. It is a consequence of the freedom of the human person, in seeking fullness outside the relationship with God. (This is the mystery of original sin.)

The presence of God in the midst of His people educated the Jews to look at reality in its truth. Job could face questions about the suffering of the innocent from within this relationship with the God who saves.

What does this mean? Can you give an example?

Years ago, in a gathering with students from the school where I taught religion, one of them arrived very angry because one of his friends had had a car accident. "How can God permit evil?" he blurted out as soon as he finished telling about the accident. I began to answer him that the true challenge was not that these things happen but how we face these facts. To help him understand, I asked him, "If walking home today a total stranger came up to you and slapped you, how would you react?" "I'd slap him back, harder!" "But what if when you arrive home your mother slaps you?" I was surprised at how he understood the question. "I would ask her why." "The slap is the same thing, materially, so then why would you respond differently? Why didn't it occur to you to respond to your mother the way you would have responded to that stranger? The reason is obvious: the relationship you have had with your mother for years and years. The certainty that she loves you prevents you from repaying her in kind and motivates you to ask her why she slapped you." This episode made me understand that what truly makes the difference when facing pain is how each of us comes to it, what experience we have in our past that conditions whether we react in one way or in another.

What enables us to look at everything, even evil, even the things we do not understand, even things that frighten us, even the things that are uncertain when the earth shakes because of an earthquake? Having experienced a relationship with God enables us to look at everything, even evil, with His presence in our eyes, without fleeing and without succumbing to recrimination. If that bond constitutes how we face everything, we can even face evil without despairing, as the people of Israel have shown us. Precisely in that moment of crisis, when the Israelites are stripped of everything and driven into exile, they show that through their relationship with the God who chose them, it is possible not to censure evil. In this way, the people of Israel come to an awareness that everything that happens during the experience of exile is for its purification; everything happens so this people can understand who God is and return to Him with a simple heart, to resume the road in a different way.

Those who are familiar with Him can ask the most shocking
questions, as Job does, without being dominated by suspicion
of God. The Father did not even spare Jesus suffering and
death. I have often wondered how evil, pain, and suffering hurt
us. It is evident that when someone wounds us, we immediately sense detachment from that person, and suspicion worms its
way in, creates a separation. The deepest harm is introducing a
separation into a relationship with another. In Jesus, instead,
evil could not break His bond with the Father. It is interesting
that the dialogue in the Garden of Gethsemane was not a com-
plaint about Pilate, Herod, the Sanhedrin, the high priest, or
the Pharisees. The content of the dialogue with the Father concerned His design. "Father, if You are willing, take this cup
away from Me; still, not My will but Yours be done."[10] And the
dialogue culminates in that crucial moment in which Jesus, on
the cross, asks the Father the true question, "My God, My God,
why have You abandoned Me?"[11] Here we truly see how pain
does not break Jesus's bond with Him. "Father, into Your
hands I commend My spirit."[12] Jesus reveals in that moment
the true reason for delivering up His spirit to the Father: "The
world must know that I love the Father and that I do just as
the Father has commanded Me."[13] This is the triumph of the
bond, the sonship, the constitutive relationship with the
Father, precisely at the culmination of His suffering. The victory of that bond is seen even in Jesus's gaze on those who mock
Him – "Father, forgive them. They know not what they do" –
and it is what shines forth in the resurrection.[14]

The victory of Christ, that is, His resurrection, is the one adequate answer to evil, suffering, and death. In the companionship of the risen Christ we can enter into any darkness fear-
lessly, like a child holding his mother's or father's hand. We can
face the unbearable horror of the Shoah, raising our cry to
God, as Benedict XVI did years ago at Auschwitz. "Why, Lord,
did You remain silent? How could You tolerate all this?" but
always with the certainty that "even though I walk through the
valley of the shadow of death, I fear no evil; for You are with
me."[15]

The whole problem of life is how to remain in the certainty of this relationship. In fact, in the final analysis, the thing that is tested in sickness, misfortunes, situations that overwhelm us and disturb us (in this period I am thinking of the phenomenon of terrorism and the fear that it generates), is precisely this certainty. When we find ourselves facing certain circumstances, we wonder, "Will this bond continue to hold? Will it be enough to face this situation, too?" Nobody can answer better than Saint Paul, who was spared no tribulation. "What will separate us from the love of Christ? Will anguish, or distress, or persecution, or famine, or nakedness, or peril, or the sword? ... No, in all these things we conquer overwhelmingly through Him who loved us. For I am convinced that neither death, nor life, nor angels, nor principalities, nor present things, nor future things, nor powers, nor height, nor depth, nor any other creature will be able to separate us from the love of God in Christ Jesus our Lord."[16]

Faced with the theme of the evil in the world, and even more faced with the suffering of the innocent, the suffering of children, we feel our entire being challenged and uncertain. If you are truly sincere, you know you are incapable of giving an explanation, especially if you find yourself facing certain situations. There are moments when nothing you can say seems congruous or adequate. Nothing you can say is suitable. All formulas, even doctrinally correct ones, are distant and seem incapable of wholly embracing the enormity of the drama that is happening. It is as if a discourse, any discourse, even a Christian one, appears inadequate. I was very struck on Good Friday 2011 by Pope Benedict XVI's answer to a seven-year-old Japanese girl, Elena, who spoke to him about the tsunami and the suffering she had seen happening all around her. The pope did not give her a prepared answer; rather, he said there was no answer. Here are his words: "Dear Elena, my heartfelt greetings to you. I also ask the same questions: why is it this way? Why do you have to suffer so much, while others live comfortably? We do not have the answers, but we know that Jesus suffered like you, innocent, that the true God who shows Himself in Jesus is at your side. This seems to me to be very important, even if we do not have answers, if sadness remains: God is on your side. Be sure that this will help you. One day we will also be able to understand why it was this way."¹⁷ Here you have it, then. It is beautiful that the pope says, "We don't have answers," also because any response in mere words would not be adequate to the dramatic nature of the question. The same thing happens today with Pope Francis, who more than once, encountering children with cancer, has said, "There is also a question whose explanation you do not learn in catechism. It is the question I often ask myself. Many people ask, 'Why do children suffer?' And there are no explanations. This, too, is a mystery. I only look at God and ask, 'But why? And looking at the Cross, 'Why is Your Son there? Why?' It is the mystery of the Cross."¹⁸ It is as if faced with evil, and above all the suffering of the innocent, one has no answer to give in the sense of the logic of the discourse. The only human thing you can do is not talk but embrace and feel yourself embraced, which deep down is what God did. The answer God gave to human suffering is that Christ shared it. He did not eliminate it.

This is crucial. I remember, for example, how much suffering we have had in the Church because of the issue of pedophilia. It made me reflect on Pope Benedict's letter to the Church of Ireland. Pope Francis has also returned to this often, because we find ourselves facing an enormous drama that is profoundly disturbing. It seems that any answer is absolutely insufficient.

The theme of evil leads to the theme of justice. What justice is possible in the face of evil?

Nothing seems sufficient for victims in the face of the evil done to them, not even a prison sentence for the perpetrator, which can never restore that which was wounded forever; for the guilty, it seems that nothing can make up for the harm done, when they finally realize what evil they have committed. There is no answer to the abyss of suffering experienced, nor is there any answer to the demand for justice it prompts. For the victims, everything seems little, insufficient for repairing the evil to which they were subjected. Who or what will give them justice?

What is the relationship between mercy and justice? Every time one talks of mercy, there are those who say, "Right, mercy, mercy. However, justice ..."

The need for justice cannot be satisfied by partial answers. It demands the totality. Therefore, without the prospect of a "beyond," there can be no true justice. I was struck by the final words of an interview with the philosopher Paolo Rossi a few years ago, published in *Corriere della Sera*: "I don't care at all about the proof of the existence of God. However ... there's one thing I can't stomach: I can't willingly accept the idea that the butcher and the victim both disappear together into nothingness."[19] In other words, if the butcher and the victim both end up in nothingness, if everything ends with this life, there is no justice. The need for justice, like all the fundamental human needs, is limitless and demands totality. It is precisely this that we are unable to satisfy, even if we achieve all our ambitions. None of our images of justice can totally fulfil the need for justice. We find ourselves faced with something that towers over us in every way and that strikes everyone, both the victims and those close to them, because nobody will ever be able to satisfy their thirst for justice, and the perpetrators of the abuse, because nothing will ever be able to fill the abyss that the evil they committed produced in them.

So then, what can satisfy this thirst for justice?

Only God made man, Christ – that "beyond" that entered into history – with His mercy, crucifixion, and resurrection, can satisfy the thirst for justice, can answer the need of the victims and of the perpetrators. Here, the nexus of mercy and justice emerges. Without Christ the problem is insoluble. Just as nothing can truly quench the thirst of the Samaritan woman, in the same way nothing can truly satisfy our thirst for justice. The full mystery of the human person is manifested here. Without that "beyond" that makes itself present in history through Christ, who through the bond with the Father breaks the spiral of violence, you cannot begin to hope in a different world. Without the embrace of

Christ there is no true answer, neither for the victims nor for the perpetrators.

When I went to Vilnius for a meeting at the university, one of my friends had invited a professor who had many questions and was sincerely in search of answers. He asked me, "In a world like ours, with such a pervasive level of evil, such deep destruction of the human person, with the dizzying proliferation of injustice, terrorism, etc., how can Christianity think it still has something to say?" I could not respond in the abstract, nor could I just give him a pat on the back. I began by telling him about some people who had ended up in an armed terrorist group and, through their encounter with the Christian experience, were able to find themselves again, truly realize the evil they had done, and begin a journey that led them to ask forgiveness. A woman who had been gravely wounded in a terrorist attack and later found herself involved in a Christian journey said, "For years, when I woke up in the morning, my mind was always flooded with all the scenes of horror I had seen and always carried with me. But since I met you, when I wake up, the first thing that comes to my mind's eye are your glad faces." It absolutely blows me away. Who would ever have said that that woman could begin to look at reality in a different way! This impossible thing was made possible by Christianity. The presence of Christ entered her life; the gaze of Christ became carnal and historic through individuals. This is what overcomes evil in the end. That woman's anger and bitterness were overcome because the glad faces of certain friends began to appear before her eyes. They gave her a new way of entering into a relationship with herself. Many things that happen we cannot change, but a presence can prevail in us that embraces life so profoundly that it enables us to face it in a more human way, one that was inconceivable before.

I also told that professor about the experience of a prisoner who, thanks to the Christian encounter, was able to say, "I'm certainly not happy about the harm I did when I committed that crime, but I am grateful because through this bad thing I did I was able to meet Christ." In this way, people recover and reenter society. People can change deep down inside only through an attraction, through something that fills them much more than their efforts. We do not have all the perfect answers for certain questions and certain dramatic situations, but we have the fundamental answer, which is not a theoretical explanation, but a companionship, a presence, the presence of Christ. As we have seen in Pope Francis and Pope Emeritus Benedict, this is what enables us to face the horror of suffering and the enigma of pain without expecting to be able to explain it, but bearing witness to the one answer that is the presence of Christ who embraces us, who fills life with hope.

The fruit of lived Christianity is a surprise we find within. In the beginning, that woman who was in the terrorist attack felt her blood boil when people talked about mercy. "How can you talk? You know nothing about the terrible pain I have experienced!" But then, at a certain moment, the glad faces of her friends prevailed, and her life changed. The victory over evil does not begin after our death, but here and now on earth when you live a Christian experience.

This is what happened in the most terrible moments of the abyss of the Shoah, the extermination of the Jews in the Nazi camps. In the darkest and most terrible moment of history, the bottomless abyss of evil, there were people who made gestures of hope and rebirth, like Fr Maximilian Kolbe, who offered to die in the place of the father of a family, [when the Nazis chose ten prisoners to starve to death] in retaliation [for one who had escaped].

What made that act possible? The faith of Fr Kolbe, the recognition of a Presence that filled his life so much that it brought forth the flower of an inconceivable generosity. It enabled him to offer to die in the place of that father of a family, with a gesture that caused not only his companions but also the SS guards to marvel. This is the testimony of Christ in history.

This brings to mind now the recent episode of another prisoner who, after having been subjected to a humiliating body search, reflected afterwards in his cell about that unjust treatment and was surprised to find he felt tenderness for those people who had caused him suffering. "How could they do otherwise, since they had never had the opportunity to be looked upon the way I have been looked upon?" This happens today, two thousand years after Jesus on the cross said to His Father, "Father, forgive them, for they know not what they do."[20] What is the most realistic gaze on the human person, that of Jesus that happens again in the testimony of the prisoner, or that of certain observers who stop at the surface of things? We rarely consider that people are unable to live up to their full stature if they are not looked at with mercy, if they do not encounter a real embrace of their life. Jesus is the most realistic because He is aware that, if we do not have a relationship with a presence that looks at us for what we are, we know not what we do.

Are you saying that without that presence and without that gaze there is no salvation from evil, nor even the true capacity to not commit it? How does this square with the so-called evidences, the natural law written in our hearts, and the like?

We need to regain awareness of the real situation of the human person. Many times we think that others reject certain things that are evident for Christians only out of maliciousness or close-mindedness. I am always amazed at the current relevancy of the First Vatican Council affirmation that we find re-proposed in the Catechism of the Catholic Church: "The precepts of natural law are not perceived by everyone clearly and immediately. In the present situation sinful man needs grace and revelation so moral and religious truths may be known 'by everyone with facility, with firm certainty and with no admixture of error.'"[21] Therefore, we are told that natural law is not perceived with clarity and immediacy by everyone. Even more so in the current situation, grace and Revelation are necessary for human beings; only with them can religious and moral truths be recognized fully by everyone.

At times we think that everything is obvious and clear and that the people who reject religious and moral truths are simply denying the evidence. This is not so, above all in the historic situation in which we find ourselves. When Jesus says,

"Lord, forgive them because they know not what they do," He expresses, as I said, a realistic attitude, a gaze that encompasses all the historic factors of the experience of those people who are committing that evil. He is not talking about human beings in the abstract, of ahistorical humanity, but about the one human person who exists, the sinful human being. Only when you receive the grace of an encounter – as happened for Saint Paul, who before his conversion persecuted the Christians – do you truly realize what you have done, or are doing. Paul accepted the Sanhedrin's judgment about Jesus: it was necessary to kill Him because He was acting against the Sabbath rest and attributed to Himself characteristics that only God has, thus committing blasphemy. Therefore, for Paul it was reasonable to persecute the Christians. Only when another factor was introduced and he began to see differently did he realize a new meaning. On the road to Damascus, Paul found himself faced with the living Christ whom they had laid in the tomb. "Saul, Saul, why do you persecute Me?"[22] Everything changed.

Christianity is not a new moralism, but the introduction of a new factor into reality that enables a new meaning for the life of everyone, for facing evil and suffering, a factor that is the answer to the need of the heart, to the need for meaning and affection. The situation of crisis we find ourselves living can be for we Christians the opportunity to regain the awareness of what happened to us, to realize that many things of our life, like the great convictions and values, the so-called evidences, are bound to the fact of Christ. The Enlightenment attempt to detach them from their origins, from their living roots, has proven incapable of lasting over time. So then, only through the renewed experience of the beginning can those "great things" return to being real.

I am struck by that Vatican I quote contained also in the Catechism. It tells us that so much insistence on the natural law, on ethical "evidences," actually has no effect, or in other words, these evidences are no longer so evident. This reminds me of Benedict XVI's words to the bishops of Portugal in Fatima, on 13 May 2010,

"When, in the view of many people, the Catholic faith is no longer the common patrimony of society and, often, seen as seed threatened and obscured by the "gods" and masters of this world, only with great difficulty can the faith touch the hearts of people by means of simple speeches or moral appeals, and even less by a general appeal to Christian values. The courageous and integral appeal to principles is essential and indispensable; yet simply proclaiming the message does not penetrate to the depths of people's hearts, it does not touch their freedom, it does not change their lives. What attracts is, above all, the encounter with believing persons who, through their faith, draw others to the grace of Christ by bearing witness to Him."[23]

The International Theological Commission said the same in 2009, noting that in the current context, "reference to absolute objective values, universally acknowledged, has become problematic."[24] Therefore, they should be spoken of with a certain precaution, with care, with the realism of which I spoke. We Christians often seem to have lost the awareness of the cognitive value of the Christian encounter, that is, of the fact that only what we have encountered enables us to look at life, family, relationships with others, or pain in the sense indicated by values, by natural laws. If we do not start from the experience of the encounter, the others will not be able to understand what we do; in order to understand, an experience is necessary. Only through his encounter with Christ was Paul able to understand what he did not understand before, even if he had all the elements in front of him. So then, if we do not start from what has happened to us, from the encounter that we have had, by grace, we ourselves fall into the error of the Enlightenment thinkers: we think we do not need a particular story – to belong to the Body of Christ in history, that is called the Church, and that for us has taken on a precise and specific physiognomy – in order to face reality with truth.

It was thought that values could be separated from their origin, but now we realize that having done so, the evident things are no longer so evident. The problem is that often we

Christians have ended up accepting Enlightenment thought, as if the fundamental "evidences" could be affirmed and kept alive only through reason, outside the relationship with the historical fact that caused them to emerge into reality in their fullness.

One often has the impression that also in the Church there is not a real perception of how distant certain self-referential discourses sound, or certain internal disputes, in the context of the desert that exists outside the halls where the fine distinctions of theology are debated. I am thinking of the experiences of young people, and the widespread perception about moral issues, about sexuality and marriage. What can you say?

The first thing to note is the real situation in which we find ourselves. In fact, if we have a mistaken perception, we end up proposing answers that do not correspond to people's expectations, wounds, and difficulties. In this regard I like an observation made by Hannah Arendt, "A crisis forces us back to the questions themselves and requires from us either new or old answers, but in any case direct judgments,"[25] that is, from careful, well-founded consideration of the difficulties of the present. The crisis worsens if we do not grasp the experience of people just as it presents itself, if we refuse to reflect. I repeat, I am convinced that for Christians this crisis affords an opportunity to understand the nature of Christianity even better. In fact, in this desert situation, from what point can we start anew? In order to answer, I always try to look at God's action: in order to save the human person, to make Himself known and to make His newness understood, He sent His Son, who became an event in history. Mere words or a call to ethics alone would not suffice to make us understand, to change our heart at its roots and the way we conceive of things and treat them. Now, this is the great step forward the Church has made with the Second Vatican Council; it has gained greater self-awareness and a clearer perception that hews closer to the facts of what happened with the Revelation.

Beginning with the modern age, especially in recent centuries, also because of the cultural influxes that characterized our history, the concept of Revelation appeared reduced to a set of truths and precepts. Instead, starting from a renewed gaze on the action of God as it took place, as testified to us in Scriptures, the council affirmed that Revelation is not only a set of truths. It is, to use the words of the Dogmatic Constitution *Dei Verbum*, "deeds and words having an inner unity,"[26] words and actions that are intrinsically bound with each other. Only through the inner unity of words and deeds can the person be reached, no matter what his or her situation. Jesus did not prepare His listeners with a sort of preevangelization, to ready them for the Christian announcement; He presented Himself, His presence, His way of acting, His way of looking, of embracing, of welcoming. This began to arouse interest in Him, so much so that those who were a thousand miles away in terms of perception of things, in the desert of those times, began to seek Him out. The publicans, those furthest from the common religiosity of that time in the history of the people of Israel, began to follow Jesus, to draw close to Him. Why were they interested? What attracted them? Why did they, who were at the margins, or even outside the community, begin to be interested in Him?

Giussani said, "Today's world has returned to the level of evangelical poverty; in Jesus's time the problem was how to live, not who was right; this was the problem of the scribes and the Pharisees."[27] Well then, "how to live" is the question that pervades our time, and therefore it offers an opportunity to ask ourselves about and rediscover the nature of Christianity. Christianity is the event of God who enters into history and becomes human companionship for our journey to respond to that question. Only if it is proposed according to its original nature can it once again awaken the interest that it aroused in other moments of history.

I'm quite struck that all the recent popes, in a crescendo, have increasingly insisted on mercy, beginning with John XXIII, who opened the Second Vatican Council by saying, "Nowadays, however, the Spouse of Christ prefers to make use of the medicine of mercy rather than that of severity. She considers that she meets the needs of the present day by demonstrating the validity of her teaching rather than by condemnations."[28] *Up until sixty or seventy years ago, birth into our societies almost always meant coming into the world in a Christian context. Little ones began receiving education to the faith while nursing at their mother's breast. People prayed together. On Sundays, nobody worked. The simpler and poorer the family, the more common it was to always have a dish of soup ready for the poor who knocked on the door. Even the laws were more or less steeped in Christianity. A person was born into a context that was already Christian and experienced the faith before starting catechism. You understand, then, why in those years the Church worked tirelessly to preserve people from eternal damnation. Today this context no longer exists, and thus starting out with condemnations or doctrine opens no breach in the hearts of the women and men of our times. On the contrary, it risks distancing them even more. I believe this is why the most recent popes have insisted so much on mercy. It is the way to evangelize today, showing the face of a God who, before judging you, embraces you, welcomes you, and speaks of His love for you.*

If Christianity is not the testimony of a possible fullness and of a gaze on life that offers a new start, of what use is it? Who can it interest today? Nobody. Labels are useless. The true question that remains is whether there is something in reality that can be an adequate response to the problem of living.

Mercy is in the Gospels and in the fathers of the Church, but one begins to rediscover it precisely in the moment when one begins to perceive that we no longer live in a Christian society. It is as if mercy were the answer to this question: "What can truly touch the heart of the human person?"

What does Jesus do? He begins to attract those who, paradoxically, were the most distant. Bending over their wounds, as the pope would say today, He makes them feel embraced, loved, and taken seriously in their need for mercy. We have no idea how suffocated certain people in those times must have felt, when the pharisaical mentality dominated everywhere. Just think that it was forbidden to eat an egg from a hen that scratched around for food on the road to a publican's house. The publicans were cut out of society, from every context, and publicly pointed out as sinners because of their work in the service of the Roman dominators. As tax collectors they exploited the ignorance of the people, overcharging and keeping part of the money for themselves. The Romans called for bids to see who would pay the most to secure the job of tax collector in a certain area. Those who did this work had to collect enough money to pay for the bid and to cover their own expenses. [If they wanted to seek reconciliation with their Jewish faith and regain social acceptance,] Jewish law required they pay back at least a third of all they had robbed, and normally they could not afford to do so. It was almost impossible, and thus for all publicans, salvation was practically unattainable. With His actions, Jesus began to open the door of mercy to them, that is, to offer hope of salvation to those who, according to the mentality of the times, could never have it. Therefore, you can imagine how deeply this scandalized people. "What, you welcome even these men, who according to us should be rejected because of their sinful life? And unconditionally?" Does this mean that in embracing them, Jesus was justifying their sins or consenting to their mistakes? No! The opposite is true! They could change their life precisely because He attracted them to Himself, precisely because they were attracted by Him, precisely because they experienced an absolutely unique mercy, unexpected and superabundant. Mercy introduced them to the prospect of change in their life.

Therefore, Jesus begins by doing things that overturn the common mentality. Remember the calling of Matthew? He was shocked that Jesus would call him, of all people, but he gets up, gathers his things, and goes to eat with Jesus and the other publicans. It is such a revolutionary action that the Gospel uses very strong words to describe the reactions of those present, Pharisees foremost, speaking for example of "scandal." In the eyes of the Pharisees, Jesus becomes a scandal, a stumbling block for believing in God. The Nazarene explains why He acts this way: He did not come for the healthy, but for the sick. However, He does not scandalize only because of His familiarity with the last of the last. He also scandalizes because he overturns a deeply rooted religious mentality.

He smashed the frameworks, the religious traditions, the regulations.

The scandal forces Jesus to respond. The people saw Him sitting at table with publicans and sinners. Uniting words and deeds, He explains His behaviour through the parables of mercy, those of the lost coin, the lost sheep, and the prodigal son. In the parable of the prodigal son, we see very well just how upsetting his behavior was. Jesus, responding to those who were scandalized, seemed to say, "Look, I act this way because my Father acts this way. It isn't that I am unfaithful or want to subvert what you have received from the Jewish tradition. No. It is that my Father acts this way, and so I act this way because I am the son of My Father," a father who welcomes the prodigal son, that is, a son who had become not only a sinner but the worst of sinners for a Jew as he ended up tending swine, the most impure animal a Jew could think of. This is the one the Father welcomes back as his son. The comparison with the older brother is interesting, because he represents the mentality of the Pharisees. "What do you mean? I've stayed here and been good all my life and you've never even given me a young goat to feast on with my friends!" The Father answers in amazement, "But don't you realize that all I have is yours?"[29] The Father cannot understand and is shaken by the lack of openness, involvement, or love for the brother who has returned, the love that the Father instead feels, the love that caused him to wait day and night for his son.

We, too, tend to say that the parable of the prodigal son is hard to take. It seems unjust to us, to our human eyes, according to our human justice. That superabundant mercy seems unjust.

Yes, "mercy" is the word that seems unjust to the Pharisees. In fact, Jesus presents another parable that is also difficult to accept for the same reason, that of the workers at the eleventh hour. The owner of the vineyard ordered that those who came to work last, at the eleventh hour, should be paid the same amount as those who came first, at the beginning of the day. For those who worked all day, this is unjust.[30] These parables speak more clearly to us if we look at them in their historical context. Who are the last ones? Who is paid the same amount? The last ones are the publicans. The first ones are those who began right away to respond to the call of God. Instead, the last are those who were uninterested for a long time. Only with the arrival of Jesus did they feel touched. Jesus speaks words of fire to the Pharisees, "Look, the publicans will enter the kingdom of God, and you will remain outside, because they are more willing to accept Me and the newness that I bring. On the other hand, you Pharisees, who came in the first hour, are not open."[31] The upheaval has to do not only with an unheard-of form of human solidarity but also with the challenge that Christ represents for the life of the human person. Those who run up against such a gaze, a proposal like His, no matter how far off or lost they are, cannot help but sense that a chink is opening in what was formerly a closed wall. I think this is why the popes are calling us to that gaze. This means returning to the origin, to the original nature of Christianity, to how Jesus began to make Himself understood precisely by those who were apparently the furthest away.

Pope Francis could be called "the pope of mercy." Do you agree? And if so, why? I was struck thinking about what you just said because one of the accusations people make against the pope today is that he attracts and speaks the most to those who are far away, and gives the least attention to those who are close.

I think that the pope will be remembered in history for this attitude. His gaze is so irresistible that he attracts the people who are the farthest away. The thing that happened in the Gospel is being repeated. But it is something that characterizes the line of the recent popes. Paul VI, for example, in his famous speech at the close of the Second Vatican Council, spoke about the spirituality of our world and quoted the parable of the Good Samaritan. John Paul II insisted greatly on mercy and had a strong bond with Sister Faustina. Pope Benedict XVI took up the line of both of his predecessors and insisted, as Pope Francis does, on how the people of this world of ours need mercy. Francis wanted an Extraordinary Jubilee of Mercy to say, "Look, the doors are open for everyone, no matter what situation they are living in." He has done everything to communicate, 2,000 years later, this gaze of mercy that people immediately recognize. The pope is able to take simple actions that communicate the same content his predecessors did, reaching everyone. Everyone understands it through certain actions of his. It is a grace that in this time the Lord has given us a Pope who is able to communicate the heart of the faith, the Christian announcement, with such simplicity.

I was very struck that in January 2002, in his first message for the World Day of Peace after September 11, Pope John Paul II said, "No peace without justice, no justice without forgiveness." If there is no forgiveness in mercy, human justice risks being transformed into injustice because it is never finished; there can never be full satisfaction for everyone, and you will never have all you believe is your due. The attack on the Twin Towers had just happened, religious fundamentalism was powerfully present on the world scene, a new phase of war had begun, and yet Pope John Paul II insisted on forgiveness as the fundamental element for true justice.

All this has to be explored fully, to the point of perceiving it in your own experience, to understand why mercy is the one adequate answer to the need for justice. On one of my trips to Brazil I had the opportunity to meet a judge who told me a story about a case he was assigned, in which like many other times he had to judge a person for a crime. But when he pronounced his verdict, the prisoner told him, "Judge, sir, I'm not ready to go to jail." He said, "I'm sorry, nobody is ever ready to go to jail." The fellow said, "Look, I don't deny what I did, and I don't question the sentence. I own up to it. But if I go to prison immediately, it will create a bigger problem than the one you want to resolve with my imprisonment. If you grant me ten days so that I can deal with my family situation, then I'll return, go to prison, and serve my time." The judge was amazed and replied, "I'll give you thirty days!" On day thirty that man was there in front of the judge to serve his time. Almost not believing his eyes, that this man had shown up freely without the judge needing to order the police to bring him to jail, he gave him the address of the prison and that man presented himself alone. This is amazing: it seems unreal to us. Who would do such a thing? And yet the experience of the APAC prisons in Brazil, which I mentioned before, works. The statistics demonstrate that the percentage of recidivism for normal prisons is 80 per cent, while in these prisons without guards or bars, it is 15 per cent. Most of these prisoners work on themselves and then rejoin society, stop committing crimes, and do not return to prison. It is significant that this type of prison was taken into consideration in the dialogue between the FARC and the Colombian government during the peace process, for the recovery and return to society of the former guerillas. It will be a very difficult process. But without the capacity for acceptance, forgiveness, and social reinsertion, these situations have little prospect of resolution.

The theme of justice thus presents powerful questions. And, as we see, when you go deep down into the need for justice, you begin to comprehend the importance of mercy, because when mercy is absent, all our attempts will fail.

Don't you think there is the risk today that mercy will be mistaken for feel-good sentimentality? Some people say this about the pope's teaching.

I told the story of the judge precisely for this reason. Was that feel-good sentimentality? No, it was exactly the opposite. Think of the encounter with Zacchaeus. Jesus stopped under the tree Zacchaeus had climbed. He looked at him and esteemed him in a way nobody had ever done. He entered his house unarmed, without lambasting him for all his errors, without asking him to change first. This act of mercy changed Zacchaeus's life. Neither a clear judgment on the sins he had committed, nor a call to morality, nor the censure of those around him had served to make him change course. Jesus's unheard-of gesture, going to the home of the publican Zacchaeus, drew a strong reaction from people.

Everybody hated Zacchaeus. He was the most hated person in the whole city of Jericho.

Zacchaeus was surrounded on all sides by judgment of his sin, but that judgment did not make him change. Only Jesus's gaze, His gesture of going to eat in his home, could do it. So then, let's ask ourselves, is that gaze feel-good sentimentality or is it the root of the possibility of change? Often in a society like ours, this is difficult to understand. Nothing can break down our resistance and challenge our freedom like an authentic preference and freely given love that affirm us totally.

Benedict XVI reminded us that behind a veneer of apparent self-sufficiency, the desire to be accepted, embraced, and loved dwells deep in the heart of contemporary women and men, in each of us. By analogy, we see it on the most immediate human level. A man may be closed, may not give a fig about anything, may be a libertine, may focus on his own affairs, until he unexpectedly falls in love. From that moment, being seized by the person who attracted him frees him from close-mindedness, from focusing on his own affairs, from libertinism. He wants nothing more than to follow the bond that makes him more himself. There is no greater challenge to the heart of the human person than to be loved freely, without meriting it. When we say that mercy is feel-good sentimentality, we forget our own experience and that of others, the newness of life that blossoms in an "I" touched by mercy.

I believe we need to be aware of the fact that we need this mercy like we need the air we breathe. As long as we are accustomed to notice the splinter in the eye of another, as is our wont, any act of mercy and forgiveness seems like feel-good sentimentality. But when you have the courage to look at the beam in your own eye and the abyss in your own heart, then you feel the need for endless mercy. There is a page in the novel The World, the Flesh, and Father Smith *by Bruce Marshall in which Fr Smith remembers what his mother used to tell him as an antidote to his spiritual*

pride: "Always remember that you can't see into other people's souls,
but you can see into your own, and so far as you really know there
is nobody alive more wicked and ungrateful to Almighty God than
yourself."[32] *In effect, this is true. If we have the courage to lean out*
over the abyss of our "I," the only soul we can see is our own. But we
are always accustomed to judging others.

But even this full awareness of ourselves emerges only when
the gaze of Christ reaches us; then we realize how closed and
self-referential we were. What blew apart the measure Saint
Paul used to look at himself and others? A fact, the encounter
with Christ. It was so powerful that it forced him to rethink
everything he thought before, and it made him regard as trash
everything that he had previously considered worthwhile. It
brought an unimaginable gladness into his life.[33] The relationship with Christ makes possible a "more" of humanity, generates a new awareness of oneself and things, enables me to realize that I was noticing the splinter in my neighbour's eye and
what else I was missing. When I only noticed that splinter,
what was I seeing? Only a part of reality. Only when something
opens up our gaze do we then understand. As Saint Augustine
said in that splendid line about Zacchaeus, "He was looked at,
and he saw."[34] He began to see reality according to all of its
dimensions, to see himself and what he truly desired for himself; he also began to see what he had done. Only when he was
looked upon did he see, because only in being looked upon
can one see. It is useless to work yourself up into a state,
denouncing the limit of the other. If people do not feel looked
upon, loved freely, and embraced, it is unlikely that they will be
able to recognize with truth the harm they have done.

Only when we are embraced, when we are deeply moved by
the warmth of the embrace we have received, we have the
courage to recognize what we are, poor sinners in need of forgiveness. This is what enabled the prisoner I spoke of earlier to
look in a certain way at the person who hit him. "If I had not
encountered this love and this mercy, I would be like you. You
have not experienced the gaze that I have experienced. How
could you act otherwise?" Who is able to grasp with realism the

situation of the person who hit him? Only someone who has experienced a gaze of love and mercy upon himself; he can realize what the other man is missing. Having received the grace of a gaze that is finally human, that prisoner knew the key that enables a person to change and can look with mercy and love upon the guard who treated him unjustly.

3

An Exegete amidst the Cherry Orchards of Estremadura

From the Parish to Studies of the Gospel in Aramaic

Fr Julián, have you ever had doubts about faith?

Many questions, yes. Doubts that would undermine the gift of faith that I have received, sincerely no. Perhaps this is because ever since I was very little I had the grace of experiencing a familiarity with Christ that amazed me and led me to make precise choices. It is like someone who carries within the experience of his mother's love. Questions, issues, even doubts can arise, but everything is immersed in this experience of familiarity. I also realize this when problems come up, because my attempt at a response always starts from this familiarity. For me, doubts always were set in this context.

Do you mean a context of familiarity with Christ?

Yes, a familiarity with Christ, which I found within and which has never left me, also because at a certain point I decided to continue my life in the seminary, where it never ceased to grow. Then – I had already been a priest for almost ten years – another factor entered in, the encounter with Luigi Giussani, who educated me to give greater human profundity to all this. Often I would tell him, "I will always be grateful to you because ever since we met, you have enabled me to make a human journey in the faith." Being educated to use reason, as happened with Giussani, allowed me not only to respond to the questions that over time presented themselves within a climate of familiarity, but also to give myself adequate reasons, taking all questions seriously. I realized that I could no longer face doubts and darkness without using reason fully, without arriving at a clear judgment.

Nothing was excluded from this way of approaching things, not even the questions that were the most difficult to take on. Once a young man, tormented by his sins, asked me, "Deep down, what does Christ think of me?" Instead of responding by asking him what had happened or telling him to recount his life story, I asked, "What are the most powerful actions that Christ has taken for you? First, He gave you life, and even when you make mistakes, He continues to give it to you. This means that you are more important than all the errors you can commit. It is a given fact. Therefore, right now I don't care anything about what you've done. Your being here in front of me tells me that you are, you exist, and if you exist it is because an Other is making you now, is giving you life, being, now. Then there is a second fact, the most powerful of all: Baptism. When you were baptized, Christ told you, 'You are mine. I love you, and nothing you can do will ever budge me a millimeter from this love for you.' These two actions tell you what Christ thinks of you." Also here, it was a matter of using reason fully. While I was trying to explain the power of Baptism, I was reminded of a moment in the history of the Church, during the persecutions, when Christians were afraid and renounced Christ. The Church had to decide on a crucial theme: whether renouncing Christ in front of the emperor, and in front of the whole assembly, also meant cancelling Baptism. The Church said no. No denial or rejection on our part can cancel Christ's gesture to us. "Baptism seals the Christian with the indelible spiritual mark (character) of his belonging to Christ"[1] forever, as it says in the Catechism. You can understand very well what the Church says. It is like a mother and child: no matter what that child does, he will always be her son. Even if he messes up big time, he will never cease to be her son. Jesus says that if we, with our sinfulness, can behave this way with our children, how much more will He, who is the Son of God, do so for us.

*This is an example Pope Francis also quoted in the dialogue on
mercy: God remains faithful because He cannot do anything other
than remain faithful. He is God. We are the ones who are unfaithful.*

But this faithfulness of God, which is His truth, must be
acknowledged at every bend in the road. So every doubt, every
difficulty, every crisis becomes an opportunity to reach greater
certainty. I am always amazed to remember the way Jesus
turned to His disciples after He had spoken about eating His
flesh and drinking His blood, and everyone else left, and only
they remained there with Him. He could have discussed it in
many ways or worked another miracle to keep them with Him,
to seek to convince them, exploiting their feelings. Instead, He
faced them with a question, "Do you also want to leave?"[2] He
certainly was not encouraging them to abandon Him. He was
challenging them to use reason fully, so they would find in
their own experience, in what they had lived with Him, the
reasons for remaining. The others could go. After all, that day
they had gone by chance to listen to Him. But not the disciples. They had numerous reasons to remain. Thus, the moment
of difficulty became an opportunity to acquire greater certainty. The same is true for us. When I talk with young people who,
maybe while they were living a positive experience, declared
their skepticism about the faith or did not seriously face their
fears and uncertainties, I provoked them by asking, "Why don't
you go?" I remember a young seminarian who was tormented
because one of his companions had left. I asked him, "Why
don't you go?" I had absolutely no intention of pushing him to
leave the seminary. Rather, I was trying to provoke him into
finding in his experience the adequate reason for remaining.
"If you ask yourself this question this every time one leaves,
every time you are in crisis or have a problem, all this will
become an opportunity for understanding more deeply the
reasons for remaining. Instead, if in the face of every crisis you
close in on yourself and retreat, your faith will remain mere
sentimentalism, and you will be increasingly weakened by the
succession of challenges. Asking yourself this question will
force you to give yourself the reasons. Pay attention, not to

abstract reasons, but to those that emerge from the facts that led you to believe, like the daily actions that make you certain of your mother's love."

Can I ask you about your relationship with death? Does it frighten you?

The most direct experience I have had of death was when my father died fifteen years ago. I was already fifty years old, but I was surprised by the way I looked at this event. The first thing that occurred to me was to ask what the reaction of Peter, John, and Andrew was when they faced the same circumstance. I thought they could not have looked at the body of their father without having in mind the fact of the risen Christ. They had seen their friend Jesus laid in the tomb, and then they encountered Him alive. That day, I said to myself that I had seen Christ alive. I cannot think that death is the end. I cannot look at it without having in mind my experience of faith, and I expect I will always look at death this way. When we think about death, our death, the type of experience we have had and are having in life is crucial. The way we face death is the test of the type of journey we have made in life. In fact, notwithstanding the fear, notwithstanding the anguish, notwithstanding everything, you cannot rip from every fibre of your being what has suffused your life for years, the facts that have happened, the many gifts you have received, in spite of your human frailty.

Could you briefly recount the family context into which you were born and your memories of your early childhood?

I was born and spent my first ten years in Navaconcejo, in a very beautiful valley of Estremadura, Spain, a valley full of cherry trees, surrounded by farms. My father was a farmer and we lived in the climate of religiosity that was normal in Spain in the 1950s. My family was religious, both my mother and my father were, my father in a bit more sober way. My mother participated more actively in Christian life. Therefore, also because of this, I was full of an initial fondness for the life of the Church. I served as an altar boy and my religiosity began to emerge without my doing anything in particular. I just found it within. My vocation sprang up from this family, social, and ecclesial climate. As far as I remember, ever since I was little I always desired to become a priest, and not in a vague or imprecise way. Even though I was only nine or ten, when the religious of various congregations arrived and invited some of my altar boy companions to go with them, I was never tempted to follow them. I wanted to be a diocesan priest. And when the moment arrived, I entered the seminary.

What seminary did you attend?

The seminary of Madrid. My grandparents lived in the capital. Initially, however, I had applied to the seminary in my area, in Plasencia. That year the Spanish Education Ministry offered scholarships for school and I had passed the exam to get one. This circumstance was a good opportunity for me to clarify the reasons for my desire to enter the seminary. Those who won the scholarship usually went to one of the best schools in the provincial seat, Cáceres. It was a good scholarship and many of my friends lived on it throughout their studies. I could have said, "Well, now I can afford to study and I can stop thinking about the seminary."

How old were you then? What made you go from Plasencia to Madrid?

I was ten years old. For a year I attended school. I remember that after the first year, one summer day while I was helping my father harvest potatoes, he asked me, "Do you still want to go to the seminary?" I said yes. So my grandparents, who lived near the seminary in Madrid, spoke with a priest they knew, a canon of the cathedral, and asked if I could spend a few days living there to have a first contact with the Madrid seminary. They welcomed and accepted me. So I left the school I had begun attending in the provincial seat and moved from Estremadura to Madrid, where I became a priest.

Who ordained you?

The auxiliary bishop of Madrid. At the time the cardinal archbishop was Vincente Enrique y Tarancón; he should have ordained us, but he couldn't be present.

Which priests or teachers were important for your training?

Those who most marked my life were Fr Francisco José Pérez y Fernández-Golfín (who would later become auxiliary bishop of Madrid) and Fr Luigi Giussani. Fr Francisco was the spiritual director of the seminary in the years I studied theology, in the most crucial moment of life, because it is the moment of the passage to maturity. Having had him close was crucial for me and for many of us. The early 1960s was a very complicated time. The period following the Second Vatican Council had generated some confusion and many seminaries had emptied. We had the fortune to be accompanied all the way to ordination by someone strongly rooted in tradition and at the same time very open to the reality of the time.

What do you remember about Fr Francisco?

His profound religiosity. He was fascinated by Christ. I am in his debt because he increased my passion for Christ and encouraged a friendship among some companions. In those years he invited some of us to create a group so that we could share the experience with one another. He had grasped ahead of his time that one of the problems of priests would be solitude. He told us, "Begin becoming friends during your theology studies so you can share experiences when you become priests." And so it was. When we were ordained, we were sent to different places. Some remained in Madrid, while others, myself included, went to small towns in the diocese. We kept up our weekly appointment to meet, read, and comment on something together; after lunch we spoke about situations we were facing at the beginning of our pastoral experience, such as catechesis, accompanying families, and so on. All this happened within this friendship, until I encountered Fr Giussani. For me it turned things upside down, because in him I found the answers to certain challenges I was experiencing, certain difficulties that with my previous education I was unable to face.

What is the name of the town where you were sent after your ordination?

Casarrubuelos, a village that had barely six hundred inhabitants at the time. I was ordained on 19 March 1975, on the feast day of Saint Joseph, and the next Saturday I had already entered that village to celebrate Holy Week. The following day was Palm Sunday. I stayed there for three very beautiful years. At the same time, I perceived the turmoil that certain social and cultural situations provoked in me, as I was not equipped to deal with them, and this intimidated me. When I met Fr Giussani I found a method that enabled me to face every situation openly, because he invited me to compare each thing that happened, each thing I felt, with the needs of the heart. Up to then, yes, I had taken everything in, but I lacked the tools for verifying in experience the things I had learned in seminary. I had the knowledge, but I lacked a method that enabled me to verify the Christian proposal in experience, when faced with all that was happening, any type of provocation. Accepting I had to learn again what I thought I already knew made me more certain of what I was living, because I realized that everything contributed to confirming the importance of Christianity. The journey of verification generated in me a certainty of faith fully aware of its reasons.

After I finished my studies at the École Biblique of Jerusalem, my bishop, Cardinal Ángel Suquía Goicoechea, sent me to teach religion at the old minor seminary, which in the meantime had become a college-prep high school open to everyone. It was the same building where I had studied when I was little, and I found some of my old professors. The first sign of how the encounter with Fr Giussani had affected my life was the new way I began teaching. Having earned a doctorate in biblical studies, I possessed the knowledge necessary for speaking about Jesus and the Gospels, but it seemed that all that I knew had no effect on my students' mindset. After the encounter with Fr Giussani, things changed radically. I began to challenge them, because I had learned to judge everything starting from experience, and this encouraged them to participate in an entirely different way during lessons. My students were the first to realize what was happening in me as a result of that encounter.

Can you tell me how you met Fr Giussani?

We have to return to that group of seminary friends. Once we were ordained, we began working in our respective parishes but continued to collaborate, for example, by organizing events together with the young people. We did retreats, summer camps, and cultural activities. One of the priests had gone to Frankfurt, Germany, to study, and there he learned about Communion and Liberation. He had been given the booklet *Da quale vita nasce Comunione e Liberazione* [*What Life Gives Rise to Communion and Liberation*]. He read it and was so struck by it that when he returned to Spain he told everyone about it. A girl heard someone talking about Communion and Liberation and remembered she had heard of it before, having received advertising from a publishing house, Encuentro, founded by the first CL members in Spain. We found out who they were and went to meet them. This is how we began a relationship with them.

One day, the CL friends told me that Giussani was coming to Madrid, and so I went to listen to him. That was the first time I saw him. It was 1980. I met him a second time in the spring of 1984. We had learned he was coming to see some friends of the movement, and we asked to see him too, and we went. Then in 1985 we invited him to a summer course in Ávila. Fr Giussani came and the young people who participated in our inter-parish group were very struck. In the meantime, our group had chosen a new name: Nueva Tierra. Some of them asked him what they should do, and Fr Giussani answered, "Follow those who have guided you to this point." He did not ask them to join CL. At the end of that summer, during a dinner with CL leaders in Spain, we were the ones to ask, "What sense is there in doing two different things," that is, having two distinct movements, "when there is this common recognition?" So, beginning in September 1985, we started participating in the life of the movement and Nueva Tierra flowed into CL. From that time on, Fr Giussani became another fundamental priest in my life. I saw him once a year, from afar, when I participated in certain events or actions of the movement, but I began to know him more and more through his texts that arrived in Spain. This encounter determined my journey more than anything else.

Could you explain for nonexperts in a simple and understandable way the research you did with the academic group known as the Exegetical School of Madrid?

It started with the encounter with Fr Mariano. He suggested books to read and research to do, and he also taught us to become familiar with the great exegetes and a way of dealing with the biblical text that, while accepting the new exegetical methods, remained at the same time bound to tradition. I think we found in him the realization of what the constitution *Dei Verbum* affirmed as the approach to use in studying Scripture.

In that period, also in the field of exegesis, it seemed that everything was put in doubt, even the historicity of the Gospels.

A kind of suspicion of acquired findings had entered into the common mindset. Paradoxically, by facing those issues and applying the historical-critical method, we reached greater certainty about the faith. I always told my students when I was teaching sacred Scripture, "The problem with criticism is that it has not been critical enough," because unproven premises were assumed and their reasonableness was not verified.

Are you saying that historical criticism had become critical about everything except its own assumptions, which had become almost dogmatic?

Yes, we could say that, simplifying. Criticism must be truly critical. Studying the language of the gospels, we found even deeper reasons and even more solid certainties about the historical foundations of our faith. The Gospels are not a dreamed-up story, an invention without grounding in reality. Our studies contributed to show the irreducibility of the Christian fact, an irreducibility that persisted as the criticism became more critical.

That prompted my desire to continue studying, and so I went to the École Biblique of Jerusalem, where I began to do research for my doctorate. The inquiry to which our professor, Fr Mariano, introduced us was based on the Greek of the New Testament and focused on how the Aramaic-Palestinian language spoken in Palestine in Jesus's time influenced it. Some of these Greek texts were "contaminated" by Aramaic. Jesus expressed Himself in Aramaic, the common language of His people, but at a certain point His words were reported in Greek. Now, if we posit the existence of Aramaic words with their own syntactical and grammatical uses, this explains certain incongruities and certain difficulties in the Greek gospel text. For example, in Aramaic there are particles that may have seven different meanings. And thus, hypothesizing that the Greek text is a translation from a previous story in Aramaic, you understand why a sentence of Jesus's was translated with a different particle in Greek. The evangelists had to choose from the various possible meanings of the same Aramaic particle, using different Greek particles to translate it. These studies made it possible to resolve some linguistic difficulties we encounter in the language of the New Testament.

Can you give an example of this?

Let's look at the Greek text of the Letter to the Hebrews 2:9. Translated literally, it is, "But Jesus, who was made little lower than the angels, we see crowned with glory and honor through the death He suffered, so that by the grace of God He might experience death to the advantage of everyone." Right away, an inconsistency jumps out. What does it mean that Jesus was glorified so that He could experience death? The normal meaning of the conjunction *hopōs* (ὅπως) is in fact "so that." But if we assume that this is a translation of the Aramaic particle *di*, which could have the final meaning "so that" but also the causal meaning "because," the meaning of the passage becomes clearer: not "so that" but "because by the grace of God He experienced death to the advantage of everyone." We were attracted by this type of research.

But is your idea, or better, your hypothesis, that there was a context of spoken Aramaic, or that there were actual reference texts written in Aramaic that were then translated?

It was more a context of spoken Aramaic that impacted the Greek, as happens today among those who speak another language with influences from their own language. The fundamental difficulty is that we have not found texts written in Aramaic, and this is the first fact we have to take into consideration. However, we know that in cultures in which the rules of oral communication dominate and many narrations are passed on from memory, there are few differences between a written text and a consolidated oral tradition in a form that we could call definitive. For example, in certain countries, when a person arrived to tell stories that were already well known and formalized, at times, the people who listened intervened to correct the person, because it was a narrative everyone had already acquired. What is the difference between a formula, a tradition passed on orally but already fixed, and the written form? Practically nothing. Therefore, we can very well suppose that some expressions were transmitted orally. This would explain why three evangelists reporting the same words or scene use three different Greek conjunctions. It means that they drew upon something already fixed, and they came upon an Aramaic conjunction that could be rendered in Greek with three different particles. This methodology has been applied for some time to resolve certain linguistic problems that otherwise would be unresolvable but that reference to oral transmission can explain. In our case, New Testament Greek, we can clarify a number of points by hypothesizing that it is a matter of translation or adaptation of a narration passed on in Aramaic, of words spoken in Aramaic.

Does this line of research move the date of the original evangelical narration closer to the date of the actual events, or in other words, does it mean hypothesizing that the story the New Testament contains was formed and fixed before the date normally attributed to the four Greek versions?

Yes, this is one of the fundamental aspects, because it means that many texts that were thought to have been written much later could actually have been written much closer to the events they recount. The Letters of Saint Paul confirm this. They contain all the Christology and everyone now accepts and no longer debates their dating; they were written between the years 50 and 60. When Paul wrote them, he took for granted the concepts they contained, that is, he believed that the first Christian communities to whom he wrote already knew these concepts. But when and how did they learn them? In the preceding decades, in the 40s of the first century, when he himself founded these communities and made to them the first announcement of the Gospel. He had already announced and explained these concepts to them, and so in the Letters it was enough for him to summarize them. This means that when Paul began his mission, forming the first [Christian] communities in the world, he had already developed his entire theology. In fact, you do not see an evolution of Saint Paul's theology. Therefore, according to some authorities, he developed it very soon after the death of Jesus.

Studies on the language of the Gospels bring us to the same conclusion, the total opposite of the attitude that held for a long time that the early Christian community intervened in the texts considerably, that the texts were literary creations that arose long after the events happened and the witnesses were alive. The idea was that the community's insight contributed to making a snowball into an avalanche. The avalanche of the Christian announcement and the faith as they are presented in the New Testament would derive from what was just a snowball, and the prophet Jesus of Nazareth slowly became the Son of God. Thus, the Jesus of the Gospels would not be a real, historical figure but simply the literary creation of the Christian community. It is as if the Christology had developed against the chronology, because the chronology would not give space to all this creation. I am not objecting to the existence of a dimension of literary creation; presenting the facts necessarily involves literary creation. What I want to underline is that the literary creation is not invention. It did not come from the mind of the evangelists but attests to the memory of that unique historical person whom the disciples had encountered, Jesus, whom they described with a sober and clear style.

I am struck by how difficult it is to have this accepted. It seems almost as if you are touching a dogma of faith, as if one is obliged, even against the evidence of the information that has emerged in the more recent studies, to leave a great space to the community's creativity. Thus, the possibility that there was not time for the first communities to have a role in writing the Gospels is not even dignified as a working hypothesis for further research. However, what is to be done with the discrepancies and differences between the evangelists' stories?

It is evident that when we tell about something that happened, we always recount the story in the way we saw and perceived it. When putting the story down in writing, each person will do so with her or his own literary style. Let's take the classic example of an accident. If we question different eyewitnesses, their descriptions will never be perfectly identical. There will always be different details and shades of meaning, depending on the point of observation and many other factors. A story is never a photograph, and in any case, we have learned in recent times that even a photograph has its own angle of observation and does not describe the whole reality adequately. Thus, it is true that the Gospels are a literary creation, not a photograph, but the true question is whether or not they narrate real facts. The observation that the Gospels resemble other literary genres or other stories does not at all mean that they do not describe a fact that truly happened. The literary differences do not mean that the origin of the evangelical stories was not a real fact. The problem is that you have to take into consideration how these stories were born and all the factors that enabled their emergence. But beyond the more specific questions, the true great problem is how we can ascertain the credibility of the announcement, the soundness of the essential content of those stories.

The great contribution of the Second Vatican Council Constitution *Dei Verbum* is the affirmation that sacred Scripture, which is a written testimony to the event of God's self-communication to human beings, must "be read and interpreted in the sacred spirit in which it was written."[3] Therefore, only when a person encounters the Christian community that perpetuates the initial event and in which what happened in the Gospels happens again, can he truly recognize these stories as plausible. Origen, one of the fathers of the Church, says that Christians have an ability to demonstrate the faith that is much more powerful than Greek dialectic. Those who have seen the fulfilment of the prophecies announced and the power of miracles, as happened for the disciples, have reasons to support their own faith. But, Origen continues, there are not only the facts of Jesus's life, to which the first disciples were witnesses. There are also the facts that continue to happen in the life of those who follow the Verb of life.

To quote Saint Augustine again, "The volumes are in our hands, the facts before our eyes," facts that happen in the present.

Yes, Origen said that Christianity's reasonableness is something present today. The things the Gospel pages narrated evidently have historical value. But only if something happens to you in the present, something that documents in the flesh what the Gospel announces, can you truly approach those texts without suspecting they were invented. If you do not live in a context in which you see happening the things the Gospels describe, it is unlikely that you will be convinced by rational arguments alone. This is precisely what Saint Augustine said. This is and will always be the method through which you can approach the stories of the Gospels, because you will overcome your suspicion about the authenticity of what you read only if it communicates to you something that happens in the present, something you can experience.

The point of departure is always the present, otherwise the suspicion remains. All the other arguments, including the indicators of historicity, fail to let us leap the moat that has been created regarding the past. This divide can be overcome only through the power of something present, an event that is happening now, because you have to provide adequate reasons for the new gaze you see vibrating now in another person, in the present. Encountering the newness of Christianity means running up against a human difference that you cannot explain, and this makes you read the Gospel, grasping the import of what happened to John and Andrew, Peter and Matthew. Without this present event, we will read those pages as stories that are beautiful but not real. Instead, when something real happens to me, an encounter with a fascinating humanity that I could not have imagined, I can also understand that the same thing happened to the people in the Gospel, and therefore I can understand the full import of what is said there, of Andrew and John's encounter with Jesus, which brought into their life a newness without compare. This is the method the *Dei Verbum* indicates.

I will never forget one lesson when I was beginning to talk about Jesus and the sources represented by the Gospels. I went to the blackboard and wrote, "Gospels." A student raised his hand and said to me, "You don't think that by reading these we can know Jesus, do you?" "Ah, no? Why not?" I answered. "Because they were written by Christians, and so it's logical that they told the story in their own way." I began to dialogue with him, and I asked him, "So your way of being in reality is to be suspicious?" "Certainly," he answered. "I'm not naive." "It is obvious that you aren't naive," I continued, "and I imagine that this morning, when your mother served you your coffee for breakfast, you told her, 'I'm not going to drink this coffee until you prove that you haven't poisoned it.'" I remember his reaction. He was furious! "How dare you! I've been living with my mother for sixteen years!" "Well," I replied, "then this means that there are cases when suspicion is not reasonable at all. What is the difference between the way you reacted to the word 'Gospels' and the way you reacted to the example of the cup of coffee? Sixteen years of shared life with your mother! These sixteen years kept you from being suspicious about the coffee. And why do you think this way about the Gospels? Because you have not shared years of your life with the Church the way you have with your mother, and therefore you are not able to ascertain with certainty whether the facts recounted in the Gospels are reasonable or not."

I have always been struck by that page in the Acts of the Apostles describing the way the disciples chose a substitute for Judas after his suicide. The one characteristic necessary for a candidate, the one in-dispensable requisite for becoming one of the twelve was not good-ness, honesty, piety, or cultural knowledge but having been present since the beginning, having been present when Jesus preached and worked miracles. This essential characteristic of having participated as an eyewitness in the life of Jesus tells us that they wanted to recount the facts.

Christianity is communicated through facts. Christianity is something absolutely unpredictable, an event. Why did it hap-pen in that moment in that place, in Palestine, and not in another part of the world? Because of a mysterious design. But just as an event is unpredictable before it happens, it is equal-ly precise, concrete, and specific when does happen. It is what it is. It is there. It can be experienced. It is visible. For this rea-son, the fundamental requisite for becoming one of the twelve is having participated in that event, in that moment, and in that place. This is crucial for the continuity over time of what began.

And there is this very strong connection with history. I find it very striking that the creed, be it the Symbol of the Apostles or the longer version of the Nicene-Constantinopolitan formula normally used during Sunday Mass, contains a name: Pontius Pilate. In the sum-mary of the fundamental truths of faith for a Christian, together with the formulations of God the Father, Son, and Holy Spirit, bap-tism and the resurrection of the flesh, there is that one name that has been pronounced millions of times throughout the world for 2,000 years, to remember what happened in a specific moment of history. And it is remembered by naming this fairly unknown Roman func-tionary, to remember forever that Jesus suffered and was crucified under Pontius Pilate.

The Church remembers Pilate in the Creed. It has placed him in our profession of faith – even though in many ways he was an abominable character – to show the relationship between faith and history. Christianity is a fact, an event in history. How can I come to recognize it for what it truly is? What must be engaged in the journey of faith? Reading Saint Paul, you see very well the relationship between the first announcement and the verification of faith that each of us is then invited to make. It is the same dynamic that happens with Jesus, who asks His disciples, "Who do people say that I am?"[4] We think that the people in Jesus's time were spared the pluralism of opinions, since He was right there in front of them, in flesh and blood. But even back then everyone had a different opinion about Him. In the Christian community Paul founded in Galatia, some of his adversaries arrived and began to announce another gospel, different from the one he had announced. The Galatians felt tempted by this different gospel the others preached. So Paul reproved them with words of this type: "Are you stupid? Don't you understand what happened to you? Did you receive the newness of life you experience by following the announcement that I brought you or from these people who propose another gospel?"[5]

It is inevitable that there can be other interpretations. What enables us to recognize the truth? A certain experience of living empowers us to recognize where the truth lies, the foundation of our faith. Saint Paul says, "There is no other gospel than the one I preached to you, whose effects you see happening among you."[6] Jesus gave us a criterion for recognizing Him, that of the hundred-fold here below; we realize that there is something other and greater because life becomes one hundred times as much, that is, a newness happens in which we verify what we have encountered. It is like when you go to the doctor. How can you tell whether the doctor made a correct diagnosis and has prescribed the right treatment? From the simple fact that you get better and recover. If you recover, you do not need to know, to be an expert, to have who knows what scientific expertise. You do the verification quickly, in the present. Everyone can live this experience in the present, in the moment they encounter Jesus through the human sign that He uses.

It is the experience those first two had on the shores of the Jordan River that afternoon, when they encountered Jesus.

That day, the disciples John and Andrew, who were following John the Baptist, experienced in their encounter with Jesus an unprecedented correspondence to the needs of their heart, through which they perceived the truth of what was happening in front of them and in them. I think that this unity of experience is crucial in times of confusion like ours. Imagine if John and Andrew, in the encounter with Jesus, did not have all the reasons that made it rational to follow Him. Whom could they have asked for such reasons? The Pharisees? The high priest? Pilate? Herod? Nobody could have given them an adequate explanation for all they experienced with Him that afternoon. The human correspondence they experienced clearly demonstrated the truth of Jesus to them. If it were not also the same for us today, we would always be at the mercy of those who must explain things to us or provide us with a supplement of certainty extraneous to our experience. But this is precisely what makes faith fragile.

Jesus wants the disciples to believe not simply because of what He says but because of what they see happen. "If you do not believe in Me, believe in My works," He tells them. "The works speak of who I am, and what happens in you says much more about Me than what I can say about Myself."[7] This is wonderful, because in referring us to experience, He shows His trust in the human heart and its capacity to recognize the truth. Then, by grace, we are given the possibility to grasp the full import of Jesus.

And also the gift of testimony. I have always been struck that Fr Giussani, speaking about John and Andrew's first encounter with Jesus, always said that Peter's first encounter with Christ was the face of his brother Andrew who told him, "We have found the Messiah." Even before seeing and encountering Jesus, Peter saw the changed face of his brother.

It was his brother, changed, who first spoke to Peter about Jesus, who testified to Jesus. This is the same for each of us: we are struck and changed by an encounter, by faces that make Jesus present. For some rationalist thinkers, like Rousseau, there are too many mediators between us and Jesus to be able to confirm the truth about Him. It is not true. Between me and Jesus there is the face of a person in whom the reverberation of the Gospel shines out, in whom I can experience the truth I have been waiting for, the answer to the needs of my heart. Christ reaches me now, just as Peter was reached by his brother, through the changed face of a person, and you cannot help but ask, "Why are you this way? Why do you live this way?" Two thousand years later, I can experience the Word who became flesh and gave us life and continues to walk in our midst.

Without this presence of Christ in the present, the Christian experience would not be possible. What we are is not the outcome of our coherence, or an organization, or goodness or wisdom or a human technique. It is the outcome of the contemporaneousness of Christ. The fact of the contemporaneousness of Christ reaches us here and now through the human face of another person and transforms us: this is how we are challenged to embrace all the newness that Christ continues to offer us in the present. This is the nature and originality of Christianity that we are called to discover also and especially in these confused times in which everything seems to collapse. In fact, there are things that do not collapse, like the wonder we experience when we encounter a person who lives in a different way the daily life in which we are all immersed, who begins work in the morning with a different face, as some students said to a teacher, "Now you have to explain to us why you always have that joyous face."

This will always be what attracts and wins over our reason and freedom: not first of all a demonstration of the historicity of Jesus or the Gospels, but a different human presence that corresponds to the facts the evangelists recounted. This is the first confirmation that Christ is risen. I am amazed that in the beginning of his gospel, Luke writes a prologue that is an introduction to his entire work – in fact, he is also the author of the Acts of the Apostles. He explains that he has gathered the testimonies and facts and has ordered them. "Since many have undertaken to compile a narrative of the events that have been fulfilled among us, just as those who were eyewitnesses from the beginning and ministers of the word have handed them down to us, I too have decided, after investigating everything accurately anew, to write it down in an orderly sequence for you, most excellent Theophilus, so that you may realize the certainty of the teachings you have received."[8] Luke is not just thinking about transmitting what happened during the earthly life of Jesus. He is also writing to people of the Christian communities who had received the Gospel but who could not verify what was announced to them by questioning the witnesses. What is the truth? How can they be sure of what the Gospel recounts? They can be sure through something that they can verify in the present, through something they are seeing happen before their eyes and that is documented in the Acts of the Apostles. Luke is saying that the demonstration of the truth that Christ died and rose is the newness of life that you are experiencing now, the things that are happening among you. The Acts confirms the truth of the facts recounted in the Gospel and thus contribute to the certainty of those who read; they provoke them not only to trust what they are told but to acknowledge the newness they are living in the present. This is the true confirmation of the Gospel. This paradox could be experienced twenty or thirty years after the death and resurrection of Jesus, or it can be experienced 2,000 years later. Writing those things, Luke responded to a problem that is also ours.

It is like saying that today the announcement of the Gospel passes through the Acts of the Apostles lived in the present time, contemporary to us, when you encounter people who love each other and love you this way. There is no other modality.

The announcement passes through the humanity that we see reverberate in the faces of those who follow Jesus.

However, there is also the risk that the organization, the structures, the institutional forms of the life of the Church, including movements, do not always show this life.

This is the question: whether the organization and the institutional forms are the opportunity for the encounter. If a person wants a church wedding, if another asks to have his child baptized, if yet another has a moment of dejection because her husband has died and she wants to have a certain type of companionship and knocks on the door – all this can be the opportunity for an encounter, as it was for the people who approached Jesus, bringing all their questions and the dramatic experiences of life. This allowed Jesus to manifest His difference. The point is whether the Church, that is, each of us, testifies to this difference. This is not just the task of the institutional Church. It is the task of the simple baptized person who goes to work, who encounters others where their life is lived. I am reminded of the story of some mothers in England who go to the park with their children and make friends with other mothers, women who are not religious, or who have other religions; through these encounters, so apparently banal, they communicate the Christian life. There is no need to do particular things. Ordinary, everyday life becomes the opportunity to testify to a light that does not belong to us and that does not come from us but that we have received by grace. In those who follow Christ there is such a clarity, such a difference in the way of looking at reality, that Christianity is communicated simply, through absolutely normal and unexpected encounters.

Pius XII, in 1942, in the encyclical Mystici Corporis Christi, *reminded us that the announcement of the faith today, even more than in previous times, passes through the testimony of fathers and mothers.*

In fact. Today too, anyone can encounter, see, run up against a newness through the witnesses they meet. The announcement of the Gospel is transmitted in simple, normal, daily things. If the great words of faith do not pass through the events of life, they will not touch people.

Great words are far away, and great announcements often do not touch life. Instead, eating together, being at table together, is something deeply resonant with the Gospel stories. Think of how many times the Gospels describe Jesus sitting at table with this or that person, maybe with someone who was viewed with distain, and demolishing a whole series of traditions. Also, there are all the times He ate with His disciples, and the story of when He cooked for them after the resurrection on the shore of the Sea of Galilee where he had "fished" them in the first place.

Dinner, eating together, is a synonym of sharing, being present to the other, being close to the other person without demands. I remember the story a young man told about an evening in Florence, when he went to dinner at the home of an unmarried couple, friends of his. Speaking with him, they communicated all their fear of living and having children. They did not feel up to the responsibility of procreating. At the same time, however, they felt close to him, and so they opened their hearts to him, revealing their wounds, fears, anguish, and doubts. They sensed in him a difference in his approach, a different gaze on life. So, as he was saying goodbye, one of them said, "Why is it that when you are present my fear is defeated?" It can happen that by chance, a person invites someone to dinner and discovers an entirely new experience of living.

Let's go back to talking about your life. At a certain point you left teaching and academic studies on the Gospels to follow Fr Giussani, moving to Milan. Why?

I left teaching and research because Giussani asked me to come live with him, to help him lead the Communion and Liberation movement.

What year was this?

This was the outcome of a fairly long sequence of events, because beginning in the early 1990s Fr Giussani began saying that the leadership of our movement should be Italian-Spanish. All this started with some of his visits to Spain, during which he was surprised by the type of friendship we had. So, as the relationship with him slowly grew deeper, Fr Giussani began writing our cardinal archbishop, thanking him for the contribution we brought to the life of the whole movement. He asked him to allow me to come to Italy.

Who was the cardinal?

He was Archbishop Antonio María Rouco Varela. In the beginning, he responded that he understood the reasons for the request but felt that I should continue my work of research and teaching at the Facultad de Teología [Theology Faculty] of Madrid. Even though he acknowledged the value of the movement, initially he said no. Then, after a series of subsequent requests, Giussani turned directly to Pope John Paul II, expressing his desire that I be allowed to leave Spain to come to Milan and work by his side in the leadership of the movement. The pope asked the archbishop, who at that point allowed me to move to Milan.

What year was this?

It was March of 2004. Up to that point, Cardinal Rouco Varela had repeated to me, "This is what I see. And if nobody gives me another reason I should change my mind, I'll keep you here." Therefore, when he heard directly from the pope that it would be useful for me to join Fr Giussani in Milan, he changed his mind. It was the feast day of Saint Joseph, 19 March 2004. The archbishop called me and said, "The pope asked me; you can go." So, after a few months in which I split my time between Madrid and Milan, in September 2004 I moved definitively to Milan, to the Sacred Heart Institute, where Fr Giussani lived. He was very sick during that period and died a few months later, on 22 February 2005.

He was already very sick, but was he still present, conscious?

He was present, although it depended a lot on the phases of his illness, Parkinson's, and on all the complications it caused. In certain moments he was not in the best condition and it was not possible to converse with him. Even when the situation was more favorable, I did not want to burden him with too many questions. When he was better, because he had rested well or because he had a bit of respite from the pain, I saw him return to the way he was years before, with that characteristic gaze of his that ran right through you, full of profound wonder and stupendous amiability. A gaze that always remained the same up to the very end in our moments of shared life, even though we were not able to talk about many things.

Did you understand why Fr Giussani wanted you to be close to him in the last phase of his life?

This is a mystery for me and will remain so until he explains it to me himself in heaven. I do not know why he thought of me. There were many others who had more degrees than I do, more history behind them, who had shared more of his life, and knowing this made his call even more shocking for me. I remember that the one thing I could not do, precisely because of all he had meant for my life, was to say no to him. Therefore I said I was willing to answer that call, ready to give him a hand. I certainly could not imagine that shortly after I arrived in Milan Fr Giussani would die. I knew he was ill but not that his death would come so soon.

Was he the one to indicate you as his successor in leading the Fraternity?[9]

Yes, it was 27 March 2004. Fr Giussani communicated it personally to the CL national council, which had gathered at the Collegio Guastalla in Milan. For years he had expressed, also publicly, his intention to entrust me with this responsibility.[10] While I was still living in Madrid, he entrusted me with the leadership of certain activities and appointments during the summer or during some very important moments of the life of the movement and of the Fraternity. In this simple way he made it known to everyone. It was clear to everyone that this was his desire. When he died, the central diaconia of the Fraternity, which according to our statues has the responsibility to elect the president, unanimously adopted what Fr Giussani had indicated.

The first thing I did after being elected – it was 19 March 2005 – was to acknowledge that my election gave the first essential signal for the life of our movement. The members of the diaconia might have agreed or disagreed with that indication, but they honored it as a way of following Fr Giussani. They accepted his suggestion. This first signal was absolutely

overwhelming for me; people not only listened to what Giussani said, but they also adhered to his proposal. My election
passed through their freedom.

*Did you expect it? Did you expect to be elected president of the
Fraternity?*

Yes, I expected it because nobody had raised objections up
to that point. And the election was unanimous.

4

The "Perceived" Movement and the "Real" Movement

Charism and the Risks of Being Self-Referential

Fr Julián, what is a movement in the Church?

To put it briefly, a movement is a united people, a companionship created by a charism, that is, a gift the Holy Spirit gives to those He chooses in order to continually renew the Church and persuasively reach people of every time and condition in the ever-varied situations in which they live. This phenomenon has happened many times throughout history. After the fall of the Roman Empire and the barbarian invasions, God raised up a man like Saint Benedict, who, setting nothing before Christ, through his way of living and communicating the faith, generated around himself a great movement, through it regenerating the life of the Church and rebuilding an entire civilization. Safeguarding and transmitting all that was great and beautiful in the past, causing it to rise again from the foundations, the Benedictine movement enabled the birth of a new civilization that found its expression in the Middle Ages. Then God raised up Saint Francis, Saint Ignatius, and so on throughout the history of the Church. And in our times, too, our movement, even considering all its smallness and fragility compared to those great examples, is a sign of the action of the Holy Spirit.

Benedict XVI, in a memorable talk given at the Collège des Bernardins in Paris in 2008, said that the monks did not have a cultural program; they had no thought of fighting a battle for the

*rebirth of Christian civilization, nor did they intend to reestablish
a civilization. They just wanted* quaerere Deum, *that is, to love
God and pray to Him, to live with Him. And this had the
unplanned consequence of enabling the rebirth of Europe.*

Saint Benedict just wanted to live and testify to what had fascinated him. This is how he began. He had many followers,
who in turn bore witness to the newness of life that came from
following Christ. The shining example of this newness attracted people, around the monasteries the human and material
fabric of society began to flourish again, and these centres then
grew into cities. The monks restored abandoned lands to cul-
tivation, showed a way to treat each other that reestablished
the foundations for co-existence, introduced song and beauty
into the ordinary weave of daily life, and communicated an
ideal for which it was worthwhile to strive and build. They
bore witness to what life could become when you follow
Christ, and thus renewed the Church and with it, society. A
charism is given for this. Independently of the capacity we
poor creatures have to live a charism in its wholeness and original freshness, the fundamental reason for a charism is this
alone: to vivify the Church so that Christ may be known. It is
a gift given to someone for the benefit of the entire Church.
God has used this method from the very beginning. I never
cease to be amazed by discovering anew how foreign to our
way of thinking is God's way of acting. The action of another
world – in the true sense of the word – in this world. Who of
us, desiring to change history, would use God's method? The
Bible recounts that after the experience of the Tower of Babel,
when everything became confused, the call of Abraham
arrived. In response to the chaos produced, God chooses one
man. This appears entirely disproportionate to us, just as the
choice of a Saint Benedict to impact history would seem disproportionate. Instead, this is exactly what happens: Christ
brings about in him a newness that strikes and attracts others,
who feel called to share it, renewing their own life, and this
change spreads to the point of building a civilization. It is stun-

ning, all the more so if we think how improbable this method seems to our eyes.

Saint Paul says clearly that God's method appears incomprehensible to people: how is it possible that He chooses what is feeble and fragile to confound the powerful?[1] This is and will always be the paradox of Christian faith. God uses a method that radically challenges us because it is so different from how we would like to act, from what we would have done. Acknowledging this method that is so "other" to us is a daily battle for Christians, first of all in yourself, and then around you, because the common mentality goes in the opposite direction.

What is the Communion and Liberation movement? Could you please explain it to someone who knows nothing about it and is not a Church-goer?

Perhaps the best way to answer your question is to tell you how it started. Fr Giussani was on track for an academic career teaching theology. At a certain point in the early 1950s, because of a series of circumstances, among them hearing the confessions of some young men in a Milanese parish, he became aware of an urgent need that could not be put off: to communicate the faith as an event of life.[2] In fact, he observed a profound extraneousness between faith and life in those young people. Therefore, he began getting involved in the youth branch of Catholic Action in Milan and soon after asked his superiors to free him from teaching in the seminary in order to go teach religion in a college prep high school in Milan, the Berchet High School. There, he ran up against a situation that confirmed and was even worse than his initial perception. This was 1954, when the Church was still very strong in Italy and deeply rooted in the people; there were no apparent signs of secularism. Most of the young people Fr Giussani encountered came from Catholic families, went to the parish youth centre, and attended catechism to receive the sacraments, but – and here is the point – many of them were no longer interested in the faith.

The movement was born of this realization and of the prompting that Giussani received from the Holy Spirit. He was motivated by the desire to communicate the faith as pertinent to the needs of living. Why were these young people who had received initial instruction in the faith no longer interested in it? Why did they feel that Christianity was extraneous to life? Entering the Berchet High School as a teacher, Fr Giussani tried to show them the opposite, that faith is able to respond to the fundamental urgent needs of human existence. He did so through his pedagogic brilliance, his temperament, his profound passion for reason, and also his literary capacity. In seminary in Venegono he had learned from some professors, such as Giovanni Colombo, the future archbishop of Milan, to enter into relationship with literature and music. Therefore, he began to teach using what he had available – art, music, and poetry – to awaken in his listeners the awareness of their thirst for life, showing that faith had everything to do with it. In this way, even those who seemed to have battened the hatches and cut off all relations with the Church began to be interested in the faith.

As I have already mentioned, Giussani was among those who early on sensed and faced what we are now experiencing today, but at the time not everyone saw. He announced the faith to young people who had already left the ecclesial sphere, reaching them in high school and then later at the university (in the mid-1960s he began teaching at the Università Cattolica [Catholic University] in Milan), taking their questions seriously, stimulating in them a conscious and critical stance. I'll never cease to marvel at what he told his students from the very start, "I'm not here so that you can take my ideas as your own; I'm here to teach you a true method that you can use to judge the things I will tell you."[3] He meant to waken in the young people the criterion of judgment – the need for truth, justice, and happiness that constitute the heart – so that they could verify in a mature way the proposal of the faith, or in other words, grasp the correspondence of the Christian fact to their fundamental questions. Giussani sought to set each person's subjectivity into motion; he did not want them to be passive, dedicated to simply receiving a series of teachings, much less watchwords or slogans. In this way he overturned a certain way of communicating the faith, making it suitable for modern women and men, with their demand for rationality and freedom.

Therefore, the movement of Communion and Liberation – which originated in the Gioventù Studentesca [Student Youth] movement[4] – was born as an attempt to respond to a world on the road to secularization. Fr Giussani provoked young people to be protagonists and helped them rediscover the reasons for faith, proposing Christianity in its original nature: an event that enters the life of people and fulfills them. In fact, only through such an experience can the reasonableness and advantageousness of faith be discovered. To use a Gospel expression, those who follow Jesus experience the hundred-fold here below. This is the challenge that Fr Giussani issued: in the companionship of Christ, your life – when you fall in love, when you work, when you play – will be enriched a hundred times over. You will find within an explosion of life that you would never have imagined. The prize is the discovery of Jesus as a present newness that enters into the various aspects of living, in studies and also in leisure, as a fact that transforms daily life. This is also what convinces people to continue the journey. In fact, what can persuade people to follow Christ and remain Christian? The fascination of an encounter and the fact that the beauty of the beginning does not stop happening in your life, because, to paraphrase Eliot, the problem is not to lose life in living.[5] Unlike all the other things that fall away and evaporate with time, the attractiveness of what we have encountered not only does not fade away but what we have encountered interests us increasingly more, and its truth becomes increasingly evident. This is the one thing that can convince someone today to be or to remain Christian.

Fr Giussani was profoundly convinced that a faith that is not confirmed in experience, that does not prove useful for responding to the needs of life, would be unable to resist in a world in which everything else said and says the opposite. If I do not perceive the human advantageousness of being Christian, my faith will have little hope of surviving in a world that goes in an entirely different direction. Faith can endure only if it is found to be necessary in order not to lose life in living.

The movements in the Church have always caused aftershocks, as well as controversy and also some divisions within dioceses. Do you agree? Is it a natural process, so to speak? Fr Giussani began his involvement with students in the years when the Second Vatican Council was being prepared, but in later years there were many opposing positions and debates within the dioceses, for example the disputes about the relationship between charism and institution, which dragged on for a long time.

We should not be surprised about this. It has been and will always be this way because bringing something different to the status quo always provokes disturbances and aftershocks. We see it on every level and in every sphere, also outside the ecclesial world, in politics and in the economy. And in the Church it is not exclusively a problem of the relationship between the dioceses or parishes and the new movements; it is something that happens within ecclesial realities themselves. Just think of Saint Bernard and Cluny, or Saint Teresa and the Carmelite reform. When graces like this happen, there are always disturbances. When then cardinal Joseph Ratzinger came to Milan to celebrate Fr Giussani's funeral Mass [on 24 February 2005], in his homily he said, "In the strength of faith, Msgr Giussani passed undaunted through these dark valleys and, given the novelty he brought, also encountered difficulties about his place the Church. It is always the case that if the Holy Spirit, according to the needs of the times, creates something new – which is in reality a return to the origins – it is difficult to find the right direction and to attain the peaceful unity of the great communion of the universal Church."[6]

Therefore it seems to me that the challenge concerns both sides; we are all called to understand more and more that what has been given to us has been given to us for the benefit of everyone. We, too, have had to make a journey in order not to live in a self-referential way the grace we have received, as the pope reminded us in his 7 March 2015 speech. In the same way, others, or other structures of the Church have had to make their own journey to open up to the newness of the movements. But this happens over time, not from one day to the next, and so we all need patience. It seems to me that progress has been made. Also, the recent letter *Iuvenescit Ecclesia* of the Congregation for the Doctrine of the Faith stresses that in the Church, institution and charism are not in opposition, but, to use the words of John Paul II, are "co-essential." Institution and charism need each other. What better thing can a bishop do for his diocese than recognize all that is life and that is positive in the sphere of ecclesial experience? What can I do, as the leader of the movement, if not support all the new things that can emerge in the communities in the countries where we are present? It is not just the bishop's problem: it is my problem too. For example, this happened with the people of the Movimento dos Trabalhadores Sem Terra [Association of Landless Workers], with whom we became friends over the years of our presence in Brazil. What could I have done, if not welcome these new friends into the movement? After all, what did Giussani do with those of us in Nueva Tierra when he met us?

However, this assumes that new realities and movements can open up to everything and can consider themselves part of a whole that is greater than themselves.

Certainly. Every movement must understand that the grace received is given to build up the Church, the point of reference of which is the pope and the bishops in communion with him. Within every ecclesial reality, we are all called to follow the one true protagonist, the Holy Spirit who can raise up children of Abraham from the stones and makes the dessert bloom in an entirely unexpected way. We all want what is good for the Church and so collaboration is easier, even if it requires its own time to become concrete in real life. But there is more: the openness to everything is so characteristic of a charism that it also concerns the relationship with all of human reality. When Fr Giussani began to propose to the first Student Youth groups the weekly gathering called the *raggio* [ray] as a way of sharing the experience, from the beginning he said that everybody could participate in this shared moment, not just those who were already in SY. "Everybody" also meant people of other religions, such as Jews, or those in groups or parties far from the Christian sensibility. Everybody really meant everybody. The *raggio* was a way of showing how Christianity valorized every glimmer of truth and positivity in others, whomever they might be.

This was the beginning. When a principal in Milan who was Catholic said that Student Youth members, because of their substance and capacity, could overwhelmingly win as candidates in student representation associations and thus dominate them, Giussani refused, saying, "If there was even one Jewish student in that school, we could not in conscience force him into a religious association."[7] These episodes remain in mind and judge our present. The gaze upon the other that Giussani showed us and to which he always educated us was defined by these words: "You stress the positive, despite its limitations, and you leave the rest to the Father's mercy."[8] Our journey is to enable this gaze to blossom in each of us. Otherwise the grace received will not serve the purpose for which it was given: the life of the Church in the world.

If you had to summarize in a few words what it means to belong to the Communion and Liberation movement, what would you say?

It means participating in a friendship in which you experience an intensity of life you never experienced before, the fruit of the presence of Christ. If we look at ourselves with all our limits, and if we look at the friends around us, we realize that this intensity can only come from Him. As Fr Giussani said, the movement is "an event of life" more than an organization, an event in which people are invited to participate with their entire being, generating relationships of friendship that expand to the point of making history. Belonging to the movement will remain interesting always and only as an event of life, that is, as experience, as the possibility of making the human journey that faith makes possible.

Excuse me, but shouldn't this be the common experience of the life of the Church?

Certainly, it is not exclusive to our movement. The experience of which I spoke can be lived in other ways and in other situations and ecclesial realities. In a letter to John Paul II, Fr Giussani said clearly that he had never intended to found anything; he felt the need to return to the elementary aspects of Christianity, affirming his passion for the Christian fact as such in its original elements, period. We have nothing to add to this. Therefore, many people who live other ecclesial experiences and vocations can at the same time and without any contradiction participate in the life of the movement. CL's proposal has no other particularities than to call people to the fundamental elements of Christianity and the faith. It is so basic that sometimes people who meet us ask, "What, that's all? How is it possible?" Some people do not believe it. Instead, it is everything, just as what is recounted in the Gospel is everything: a unique, fascinating presence, without compare, that changes people's lives. In fact, those who live around the person of Jesus blossom. It is astonishing to read what the Acts of the Apostles narrate in passages that at times we fail to notice. For example, when John and Peter are brought before the Sanhedrin because they had begun to announce the resurrection of Christ in the temple, the members of the Sanhedrin were amazed by their boldness, given that they were uneducated, ordinary men, until they recognized them as the followers of Jesus.[9] If you pay attention to these passages, they take your breath away. The friendship with Christ caused such a humanity to flourish that even their adversaries had to recognize it with surprise. This motivated Fr Giussani to say, with one of his typical expressions, that Christianity is a subversive and surprising way to live the usual things,[10] those that often bore and burden us. He communicated Christianity to us as an event of new life. This is what makes participation in the experience of the movement interesting for me.

Recently, I heard about the witness borne by a mother whose son died in the avalanche that hit the hotel in Rigopiano, in Abruzzo. She was waiting for news together with the other relatives of the dead and wounded. That mother became a pillar of support for everyone, and when they said goodbye, they said, "Thank you, because your presence made it possible to live these days in a different way." Even the psychologists sent to help the families thanked her for the good she had done for everyone. This is the disruption, let's call it, that a Christian presence produces. That woman did not have any special merit for having been graced by the Christian encounter; the faith generated in her a more human way of looking at and dealing with everything, and the others were grateful to see her live this way.

What are the obligations of those who are part of the Communion and Liberation movement?

The desire to participate in the movement usually arises because people find in another person something that interests them. This is the same dynamic that happened at the beginning of Christianity. At work, at the university, in the normal spheres of life, people who perhaps had never thought of faith perceive an attraction in someone; they become aware of a way of staying in reality that attracts them. This comes before any strategy or project, and is something that happens by grace, something unforeseen. You are attracted and fascinated, and so you want to participate in the life of the person who fascinated you. When this happens, you begin to participate in the reality of the movement and therefore also in some actions that are the pilasters of the educative journey Fr Giussani proposed.

First of all, every member of the movement is invited to participate in the liturgy and prayer of the Church. Fr Giussani said, "The liturgy is the book of the poor in spirit," whom he defined as "those who do not invent words,"[11] but follow in the great river of mother Church, repeating and responding. We have a small book of psalms for daily use, summarized from a breviary and approved by the Church, which also contains some traditional prayers, such as the Angelus.

Adults who recognize the movement's direction as a proposal that is appropriate for their life are invited to become part of the Fraternity of CL, with the possibility of freely belonging to or forming what we call a *Fraternity group*, the goal of which is to help each other live the companionship to destiny, deepening our personal relationship with Christ and thus increasing the experience of the movement as service to the Church.

The primary action of the movement's life is the *School of Community*, which offers the opportunity to deepen awareness of what happened in the first encounter. This is a kind of catechesis on the nature of Christianity and all the development of life that begins with the Christian encounter. Everyone is invited. It begins with a personal work of reflection [on a text], and culminates in a meeting in which members help each other [with it].

There is a second action, which Fr Giussani indicated to us from the very beginning, the goal of which is to educate us to charity: *charitable work*. People freely and faithfully dedicate part of their time on a regular basis to share the life of others, starting from a need they themselves have. There are different ways to do this, such as going to visit someone who is in hospital, visiting prisoners, helping young people in after-school programs, or participating in a Caritas initiative in your own parish. These actions teach us to share ourselves and contribute to educating us to gratuitousness. Charitable work is particularly significant in the life of the movement because over time, the education it promotes has led to the creation of many works and initiatives in response to people's needs. These efforts did not arise from movement leaders' input but from people who, seeing various situations of need, tried as best they could with the means they had to attempt to answer. I am truly struck by the number of these realities, some of them well known, like the food bank, which many people not in the movement also support. You might say that the food drive has almost become the most important collective charitable effort in Italy because of the great participation that characterizes it (130,000 volunteers). Or there are works like Portofranco, which has spread to a number of cities and tries to respond to the scholastic needs of many young people through a daily after-school activity many children of immigrants attend instead of being left without any help in the neighbourhoods where they live.

There is also a third action, *the common fund*. The gratitude for what we have received even "touches" the goods we have, or what we earn, and educates us to evangelical poverty. In order to educate us to live in the memory of what has happened to us, we are invited to contribute on a regular basis a sum we freely chose. This action provides support for the movement's life so we do not need any external help. This is fundamental: we do not depend on any other resource than what the members freely give. We are free from any institution and any form of financing. The common fund constitutes a fundamental key for understanding the source of the money for the ordinary life of the movement.

Finally, there are some common actions such as the spiritual exercises (according to a formulation that varies for the different spheres of the movement: the Fraternity, young workers, and students), in which all CL members are invited to participate once a year, or the vacations for communities. All that I have described characterizes the life of what we call the Fraternity of Communion and Liberation, a universal association of the faithful that the Holy See recognized in 1982. Members come together freely to follow Christ and the Church according to the method of the founder, Fr Giussani.

For a long time the CL movement has been associated with the word fundamentalism. Why?

Christianity concerns your whole life; like a new wellspring, it influences all your actions and the way you conceive of everything, because nothing is excluded from the newness that it brings into the world. This affirmation has always been central in Fr Giussani's proposal. In this regard, he always used to quote a line by Romano Guardini, "In the experience of a great love ... everything that happens becomes an event in its sphere."[12] When you fall in love, the usual things become different, from when you wake up in the morning to when you go to work, from the use of money to that of free time. Nothing is excluded from the horizon of that great love; everything acquires a new physiognomy. If you have not had such an experience, you cannot understand. For that matter, Saint Peter said, "Whether we are awake or asleep we ... live together with Him."[13] For him, sleeping and waking had to do with the experience of the relationship with Christ. If you are in Christ, you are a new creature, a new being, which necessarily finds expression in every action; Christ becomes the global horizon from which you see and face everything. This is the fundamental nature of the faith. But here a misunderstanding can arise, which is what can be called fundamentalism. In fact, what I have said does not at all mean that faith automatically resolves economic, political, relationship, or health problems, or the like. For economic problems, you need to use a certain method and a certain approach, for health problems another method, and so on.

Once I asked Fr Giussani about this, and he said that fundamentalism means facing a problem without using the instruments that its objective nature demands, as if from faith you could deduce the instruments for facing things materially. Faith touches all aspects of my being; in experience and with intelligence I will look for the instruments and methods necessary for facing life's problems according to their objective nature. He said that those who accuse CL of fundamentalism hold a preconception, given that he had never denied the need for mediations, nor that the ways and methods by which Christians express their attitude must be dictated by the objects and spheres to which it is directed.[14]

Are you saying that Fr Giussani never denied the independence of the so-called temporal realities?

I believe these things I have mentioned leave no doubt. For that matter, there are a great many passages in his texts that express and develop this. Here is just one example: "Everything that Christians do involves their relationship with Christ. The autonomy of earthly realities is obvious, if by this you mean that each thing must be treated according to its own nature and according to the purposes intrinsic to this nature. But this

does not agree at all with the Christian faith if by this you
mean that there are spheres in which Christians can leave out
their faith."[15]

*What is the relationship of the CL movement with politics and
with the world of economics?*

The relationship with politics and the world of economics is
ideally shaped by what I have said up to this point: for a Christian, nothing should be excluded from the beauty of the
encounter with Christ. An ecclesial movement must necessarily educate people to face everything in the light of the faith,
including politics and money, encouraging members to fulfill
their social responsibilities, so that they act without presumption in line with their own skills and positions for the common good.

Giussani made the relationship of CL with politics clear on
many occasions. A living Christian community has a political
impact first of all because of its very existence, inasmuch as it
occupies a certain space and involves a public expressivity that
influences the social fabric of which it is part. (The Benedictine movement is a very strong example in our European history.) Secondly, because of the newness of life that develops in
an authentic Christian community, it cannot help but tend to
have its own judgments and ways of facing everyone's problems, which it offers as its specific contribution to the social
body. Just think of the challenge of education, the family, the
emergency in employment, poverty, and the various forms of
marginalization, all themes in which the Church is on the
front lines today, in continuity with Catholic social doctrine.

In this regard, I think the words of then president of the
Republic Giorgio Napolitano at the 2011 Meeting of Rimini
are significant. He defined our reality as "a human resource for
the nation."[16] President Sergio Mattarella underlined the same
thing at the 2016 Meeting, saying, "You are a precious resource
for our society."[17] This is the acknowledgment that the Christian community constitutes a good for the *polis*, an essential factor for its construction.

But while the direct action of the Christian community includes involving people in political and cultural activity and animating that activity, the Christian community as such is not engaged in political militancy in the strict sense. Giussani was always clear on this point; at this level, it is no longer the community as such that is engaged, but lay Catholics who, because of the education they have received, take on a personal responsibility, using the instruments proper to politics. This is why he said it was neither correct nor fair to define those members of the movement who engage in politics – in the ranks of a party, in a local administration, or in parliament – as CL candidates, CL politicians, or CL leaders.

Having educated people to be concerned about everything, Fr Giussani stimulated members of the movement to participate in political life. But individuals make party choices and take responsibility for them personally. For this reason, Giussani insisted forcefully that there should be an "irrevocable *critical distance*" regarding any political choice, so that a decision a CL member active in a party made would not automatically become the movement's choice. In fact, if that happened, "The ecclesial experience would end up being exploited, and the communities would be transformed into pedestals and cover for decisions and risks that instead must necessarily be personal."[18] The same holds for social works and businesses.

In recent years I have seen more willingness on the part of the media to respect these distinctions and avoid the confusion that held sway in the past. I have noted that Fr Giussani's concern has to some extent passed and that many acknowledge our efforts at clarification. I have observed an interest in CL as such that only five or six years ago would have been difficult to even imagine.

To summarize, the things that CL chooses to do on some issues such as freedom of education, it does directly as a movement. Regarding strictly political themes on which there can be different opinions, there is space for individual free choice.

CL does not enter into this. As Cardinal Ratzinger said, in the sphere of politics, "The one single correct political option does not exist."[19] Therefore, to contribute to the common good, members can take different roads. For this reason, a healthy pluralism is fundamental. "It is not the Church's task," nor that of an ecclesial reality like ours, "to set forth specific political solutions ... to temporal questions that God has left to the free and responsible judgment of each person."[20]

In spite of all you have just said, honestly, don't you think there was too much intermingling? Is it just the fault of newspapers and journalists who do not understand, or were there attitudes and beliefs, often in big and complex realities like Milan, where important men from the ranks of CL had great political and economic responsibilities?

It seems to me that the past or present existence of these risks is part of the dynamic of people's engagement in reality. It is normal that those who work in the field run risks. We may have made mistakes or had attitudes that were not adequate, but as soon as I could, I did not fail to admit this publicly, without forgetting the merits of the many people who work for the common good, subsidiarity, and solidarity.

No human institution, be it related to the Church, politics, or labor unions, can eliminate the risk to people's freedom. Each of us is personally responsible for what we do.

What I was trying to say in my previous question was not only related to the most glaring facts or the problems with the judiciary that exponents of the movement have run up against. I was also referring to the idea, very widespread in various spheres, that CL or CL members act in some way as a lobby, favoring their friends and trying to gain certain positions. This is a widespread idea, independently of the judicial problems or inquiries that have ended up in the newspapers. How do you explain this?

This is a permanent temptation for each person, as Pope Francis warns us constantly. However, I would like to stress that when this happens, it is not as a consequence of the movement's original perspective on life. From the very beginning, Fr Giussani had no intention of teaching his students to seek dominance and hegemony but to pursue a gratuitous presence. He did so by educating to a boundless desire for good that would motivate works that served people's needs and political engagement that valorized creativity from the bottom up. He repeated and stressed this many times throughout the history of our movement, trying to correct those who thought that the problem was to gain certain positions. The risk existed, and in some cases what he was concerned about happened. He saw in this attitude a yielding to the temptation to identify the Christian event, which is the fruit of an always unmerited grace, with a project that sees us as active agents. This identification is as far as it could be from Fr Giussani's mindset, and in fact he constantly corrected this temptation, always with respect for the person's freedom. Obviously, the correction did not negate the fact that the movement is a reality present in public life and as such can make a contribution in many situations. But this must always happen without any ambition to achieve hegemony.

In the intense years of contestation, Fr Giussani criticized the attitude of certain exponents of the 1968 protests in their project to change society and that of certain university students in the movement who remained faithful but adopted the same behavior, simply in reactive terms. While Giussani defended that which was genuine in the demands for change in the 1968 effort, he recognized the presumption to impose the new, or in other words, one's own project, burning the bridges with the past, placing oneself as the "measure of all things," disqualifying anyone else who had a different position. The theme of hegemony came up. In a talk in 1972, he said, "It is the naivety of the man who says, 'Get out of the way and let me set things right' ... What melancholy! ... What melancholy we felt right away in the face of society's will to change."[21] He was referring to the overall attitude of those who promoted and participated in the movement during the 1968 protests, but this naivety and presumption also characterized, albeit in different terms, the position of some people who, having remained in the movement, tried to overcome the confusion

and bewilderment the events provoked by throwing themselves headlong into an effort and pretension to change things
with their own strength, exactly like the others. Thus Christianity was reduced to moralism. Everything still revolved
around the human measure, the aspiration to build an alternative project that would be better than those of the others,
desiring to some degree to achieve Christian hegemony. In
1976, Giussani returned to these things in a firm way; we cannot have a reactive position, seeking any kind of hegemony
through which we think we can change things. If God so
desires, the change will happen on a timeline that is not ours,
if we live the event that has happened to us and are witnesses
in the world to an original presence, through acts of real
humanity, that is, charity.[22] A new reality is not built through
our discourses or organizational projects but through the true
accent of a presence generated by faith.

*So are you saying that CL does not and should not have any nos-
talgia for the* ancien régime, *no longing for the time when there
was this hegemony of the Church and Christianity?*

Giussani never longed for a return to something like the
ancien régime or a certain type of past. Just think of his emphasis on the importance of freedom, which is typically modern;
it is the value dearest to modernity. Even before the Second
Vatican Council, he held that the Church needed nothing
more than the powerful attraction of Christ, reverberating in
the lives of people fascinated by Him. This is what can truly
challenge the reason and freedom of the human person. Giussani already realized in the 1950s that the Church would be
unable to attract people except through the beauty of a life
shaped by the encounter with Christ. As I have already
observed, he had this intuition at a time when all the important Catholic associations were chock full of members and
almost nobody perceived or foresaw what was beginning to
happen, that is, the process of secularization.

*What is morality in politics and the business world? For a long
time, especially in the 1980s and 1990s, the movement criticized a
certain kind of moralism, that of people who insist so much on*

defining themselves as honest that they seem immune from making mistakes and from sin, people who divide the world into the honest and the dishonest, always placing themselves on the side of the honest. Thus there was this criticism of a certain moralistic attitude. Don't you think that in some way this ran the risk, because of the way some people perceived and lived it, of accepting and justifying behavior that was, to put it mildly, free and easy, and sometimes truly immoral, also by members of the movement or at least considered close to it? Almost as if the good of the work, and in some cases one's own business, justified everything, and as if the end, which maybe also included some benefits to society, justified any means. In this way, any objection raised about the means for obtaining a certain end was countered with "You're moralistic!" Moralism, as an attitude, is not good. However, morality exists.

Morality in politics and the business world is not different from the morality necessary in any other human activity: a striving to live according to the truth. But as soon as you say this, you become aware of the disproportion or contradiction that Saint Paul so well expressed: "For I do not do the good I want, but I do the evil I do not want." Out of this painful experience gushes the cry that each of us recognizes in ourselves: "Miserable one that I am! Who will deliver me from this mortal body?"[23] In this sense, moralism is the promethean attempt to resolve this drama by your own strength. Each of us can verify the success of our attempt. Therefore, I think criticizing moralism is more than justified. It is a different thing to use this human incapacity as an excuse for your own mistakes. For this reason, when painful public facts occurred, I wanted to clarify that they were not at all justifiable. So what is to be done? The pope says clearly, "It's difficult to do good in a society without getting your hands or your heart a little dirty; but that is why you go ask for forgiveness, you ask for pardon and continue to do it. Don't allow this to discourage you. 'No, Father, I don't do politics because I don't want to sin.' That's not good! Go forward, ask the Lord to help you not to sin, but if you do get your hands dirty, ask forgiveness and go forward!'"[24]

I think that refusing to try because you do not want to risk sinning is the attitude of those who prefer watching a game from the stands to playing on the field. Certainly, those who do nothing cannot make mistakes, while those who act always run a risk. But what is better, running the risk of making mistakes and doing something, or not making mistakes and doing nothing? Faced with so much destruction, the Christian cannot stay on the balcony watching reality. "Do I, a Catholic, watch from the balcony? You can't watch from the balcony! Get involved! Give it your best. If the Lord calls you to this vocation, get to it, engage in politics. It will make you suffer, it may be an occasion for sin, but the Lord is with you ... Do not forget what Blessed Paul VI said: politics is one of the highest forms of charity."[25] From this point of view, I repeat, out of fairness, it is necessary to also remember the many positive attempts that have benefitted the common good.

If I may be allowed, perhaps one could say that it is always important to engage and risk but also fundamental to acknowledge your own mistakes. Also, it is important not to justify the mistakes, absolving yourself and maybe branding as moralists those who point them out.

For this reason, I asked everyone's forgiveness when I wrote the public letter on the first page of *la Repubblica*. It was 1 May 2012. "Reading the newspapers these days, I have been filled with an inexpressible pain at seeing what we have done with the grace we have received. If the Communion and Liberation movement is continually identified with the attraction of power, money, and lifestyles that have nothing to do with what we have encountered, we must have given some reason for that."[26] I had no intention of justifying what had happened, nor of condemning people or putting myself in the place of those in authority. In fact, on that occasion, I also asked forgiveness if, with our superficiality and lack of following we had harmed the memory of Fr Giussani, well aware of the need we all have for the mercy of Christ. Christ is not defeated by our defeats; for this reason, we can start again, always begin again from our ashes, as if shorn of everything, and our mistakes become a powerful call to purification. Christians feel their absolute inadequacy compared to the gift given, and the Church always invites them to take the most important action at the beginning of the liturgy: asking forgiveness. Fr Giussani always used to say that there is no true human action if it does not begin with the awareness of being sinners.

Perhaps for this specific situation the words of Pope Francis are suitable, when he distinguishes between sinners and the corrupt; sinners, yes, because we are all sinners. But sinners are people who recognize they are such and get up again, asking for forgiveness. They do not justify themselves but humbly acknowledge their errors and need to be helped and forgiven. In contrast, the corrupt make their sin a system, a mentality, and in the end justify it, no longer considering it a sin. Thus immorality is justified in all fields.

It is the presumption of people of every era: to erect their own limit as the measure for their relationship with themselves, others, and all of reality. This means justifying the exploitation of the other to achieve a power that allows no limits. For this reason, I said that becoming aware of your own sin is crucial for Christian life.

What is the Compagnia delle Opere [(CdO) Companionship of Works]? Why do many people see it from the outside as a sort of business committee, even if a bit masked?

In a strongly individualistic world like ours, the Companionship of Works seems to me to be an attempt to help and support each other as women and men and as citizens trying to promote a precious good that we all desire: work. It is simply a way for people to help each other in the spirit of the Church's social doctrine, according to the principles of solidarity and subsidiarity, so necessary above all today in a context dominated by what Pope Francis called a "culture of waste." I seem to understand that many people who do not come from the experience of CL are associated with the CdO and find its activities and initiatives helpful for the survival and development of their firms, a place to share concerns and exchange experiences in a very rapidly changing world. There is always a risk that someone may act in a dubious way, as I said before. But the goal remains the one I indicated.

In any case, the fact that people who have encountered the faith want to create businesses that provide the opportunity to work, above all to young people, and to help each other face the burden of the risks and uncertainties that this entails, does not seem to me to be a disadvantage for society, particularly in this moment, given the many economic and employment difficulties. Equally or perhaps even more significant is the fact that many have desired to generate works to help those who live in situations of impoverishment. Think of the Food Bank, which I spoke of earlier, and many social works and initiatives that offer free assistance in finding work or making up serious academic deficiencies. Because of all this, it seems unjust to look at this reality only with suspicion.

Certainly, those who engage in generating this type of work must always be vigilant, guided by realism and prudence, in order not to yield to the presumption of acting beyond their own means. The need is so bottomless that when people initiate a work in response to the problem of drug addiction, or an after-school activity, or an initiative for migrants, they can easily think that what they do is too little, begin to presume they can respond to all the need they encounter, and end up overdoing things. But at a certain point they will no longer understand whether they are still trying to respond to a need or are just affirming themselves. I always say that if the Mystery gives us the opportunity to do three things, we should not settle for two and a half. And if He does not enable us to do more than three, we should not try to do five or six, because we will become presumptuous and we will err. Jesus did not heal all the sick people in His time, even though He could have done it. He could have solved the problems, but He did not do so. What does this say about our way of facing the needs we meet? This does not mean settling. It does not mean we are called to do less; rather, it means seeking not to go beyond what the Mystery allows us to do.

Thus the idea that the Companionship of Works is the economic arm of CL is mistaken?

Nothing could be further from the truth. I want to emphasize this. The responsibility for the works belongs to the individual. This or that work belongs to the person who does it, just as the Companionship of Works belongs to those who do it. It is worth pointing out that the movement does not have works, and no work is under its direct responsibility. Thus the CdO is not a work of CL. CL totally esteems and respects people's freedom and encourages them to personally take responsibility for their actions. For that matter, legally speaking, the CdO is a free association whose national and local leaders are elected and respond to their membership alone.

How does the movement support itself financially?

As I said before, the movement depends exclusively on the common fund, that is, on contributions freely donated by its members. We do not need anything else to support the life of our communities and the various charitable, missionary, and cultural initiatives. This enables us to be free from everything and everyone in carrying out our task as a movement. As an ecclesial reality, CL is absolutely autonomous from any type of entanglement with economic or financial activities. In fact, the movement only owns the central offices in Milan, the Istituto Sacro Cuore [Sacred Heart Institute] (the one school Fr Giussani wanted, to offer an example of education according to the Christian ideal), the offices of the CL international centre in Rome, and the structure that hosts the Seminary of the Fraternità sacerdotale dei missionari di San Carlo Borromeo [Priestly Fraternity of the Missionaries of Saint Charles Borromeo], in the capital as well. Period. Fr Giussani had the opportunity to receive in donation various entities like universities, schools, and hospitals, but he never wanted to accept such offers. Often he did his utmost to support this or that entity, but the ultimate responsibility and ownership of those entities never passed to CL. Giussani had no desire to increase the movement's holdings. We have nothing and we ask for nothing; this is our freedom.

Another theme I would like to reflect on is the more ecclesial side. This has been the subject of many arguments in the past, and also of many disputes, regarding the relationship between parishes and the so-called presence of the new movements in different spheres. During the 1987 Synod of the Laity, Fr Giussani had a very civil discussion with Cardinal Carlo Maria Martini, who said, "Don't think that the parishes are like old wineskins." Have that season and that conflict ended? Today, observing the reality, one might say that we are living a different season. This debate seems quite dated; time can be wasted arguing, while more and more people abandon the Church. What is the value of parishes today?

At times the evolution of history settles things in their place. What is the perennial value of the parish? As the word itself says, being situated locally, close to where people live. But as the history of our movement from its birth demonstrates, many people no longer find it in the parish, because of the radical changes in lifestyles and the growing secularism of society overall; instead, they meet the movement at school and university, in workplaces, in their free time, or in neighbourhood gathering places. I believe that the pope's call to a "Church reaching outwards" concerns everyone – parishes, movements, and associations – because we all are tempted to close in on ourselves, to be self-referential, closed in our "orchard" or our parish youth centre. The true question is whether the spheres of ecclesial belonging – parish, movement, or association – can generate people who are adult in the faith, so that through them and their witness, others can see and touch another way of living. The sphere is crucial, because we cannot cheat there. People see us there every day, when it snows, when it is hot, when there is a difficulty, when we are sad, when life is burdensome, and everyone can observe whether our way of living is more human and eventually ask themselves what makes it so. I think the controversy between parishes and movements is totally outdated. The problem is whether the spheres of belonging constitute places for generating adults who live everyday life in a different way, because Christianity can become interesting only through the testimony of such a difference.

For this reason, it is in our best interests to go out and face situations, to go out to meet people on their way (How many times has Pope Francis said, "Go out"?) in order to verify the faith, to gain a mature awareness of the gift that has been given to us, and to experience all its fecundity. To verify whether what I live in a parish or movement truly serves me, I look at reality: my studies, work, relationships, difficulties, the position of others, their objections, expectations, and problems.

Therefore, there is no use spending too much time on this discussion. We must show how faith is important in everyday life; this is the great challenge in front of us. In fact, as Fr Giussani said, it is understandable that someone may have no interest in eternal life, because that person has no imagination, but all of us are interested in living better now, in being happy and fulfilled, in the hundred-fold here below that Jesus promised us and that precedes eternity.

The movements became protagonists of the new evangelization during the pontificate of John Paul II. The presence of movements was already seen in the mid-1970s with Paul VI, as they filled gaps left by the decline of a certain traditional engagement in associations, but it was with Pope John Paul II that they became protagonists. Does being considered the "crack troops, the vanguard, the elite" at times make the movements feel a bit like they are at the top of the class?

This risk exists. But for certain aspects, we can even hazard saying that this was the divine method in action. We see it in the way the Mystery acted with Abraham. Beginning the history of revelation, God did not call everyone indistinctly: He called Abraham. His was an election, a choice. He began by choosing one man so that through him His word, His message, could reach everyone. The method that God uses to make Himself known to and recognized by women and men is to choose a few, so that through them the others will realize and understand. If they are sincere, those who through no merit of their own find themselves chosen, live this call with gratitude and wonder, as shown so masterfully in Caravaggio's *Calling of Saint Matthew*. Matthew is amazed at being called. Everyone knew him as a sinner. "Me? Are you sure? You're calling me?" he seems to be saying to Jesus. This is the attitude of those who are aware of being called, or better, of being a nothing who is called. This is hardly the attitude of the top of the class! Rather, it is like being the last in line and embracing the choice for what it is: an unmerited grace. When this awareness is lost, you succumb to the thought that you are the top of the class, the one cure-all for the Church, and in this way, you end up not being a proposal for anyone.

Do you see in CL and the other ecclesial movements the risk of self-referentiality? I refer above all to the fact that sometimes one observes that the different ecclesial entities have difficulty working as a network. At times I would say that an action, even if it is not perfectly organized, even if it is a bit slip-shod, is worth a thousand times more if it is done together, as a collaboration among various realities, ecclesial and non. It is worth a thousand times more than a very beautiful, perfect act that is invented and achieved by only one entity.

We have already spoken about this. By its very nature, every charism functions within the totality of ecclesial life; it is given for shared building and, precisely because of its specific identity, is open to the recognition of all the other charisms. The confirmation of a true charism, therefore, is that it opens to everything, that it does not close. As a sign of this boundless openness, I am always amazed to think of the beginning of the movement. As I have already said, Giussani conceived of the act of the *raggio*, where something that happened or an issue was discussed, as a moment of dialogue open to everyone, Christians, believers of other faiths, and non-believers. He had this sharp and simple perception: Christianity, when it is lived in its authenticity, is a positive and open gaze on everyone and everything. In the course of our history, every time that gaze faltered, Fr Giussani always corrected us. Not only was nothing further from self-referentiality than an act like the *raggio*, but there was also the charitable work in the Bassa milanese [the poor rural area south of Milan], a sharing in the needs of poorer people that involved hundreds and hundreds of high school students. There were also cultural activities. This is the case today as well. For example, there is the Meeting of Rimini, a meeting place for people of the most varied cultural backgrounds. A charism opens wide to the totality. Therefore, only a lack of faithfulness to the charism can make us close in on ourselves in self-referentiality.

I have to insist on this: if we do not want to deteriorate into self-referentiality we must constantly call each other to the truth of the charism, which by its nature is totalizing and catholic, totalizing inasmuch as it tends to shape all our relationships and catholic inasmuch as it opens us to embrace everything and everyone.

The more the awareness of what has happened to us grows and develops, the more this opens us to collaboration, not only with other ecclesial realities, but also with other subjects and realities outside the Church.

In the 1970s and 1980s there was considerable controversy about the modalities of Christian presence in society. So-called "religious choice" was contrasted with militancy. Today, what remains of that season, and what does it mean today to be a presence? I ask this not only because it was a controversy in the past but because today as well, some people in the movement accuse you of making a "religious choice" and not a sufficiently militant choice.

We return here to the crucial question, that is, the nature of Christianity. It is necessary to understand whether Christianity is simply something that concerns an aspect of life, or its totality. If an event is truly significant for life, it involves everything. "Whether we are awake or asleep" as Saint Paul says.[27] I think this is the question. What do we mean by "religious choice"? If we mean relegating Christianity to some religious moments such as prayer and liturgy, without the fact of Christ involving all of life, I do not agree. If instead that expression means that Christians in the world do not live as fundamentalists in the sense described earlier, then I agree.

I want to pursue this, and I'll clarify my question. Perhaps the current controversy concerns the debate between a testimony that

*passes primarily from the person, and a testimony that ends up
entrusting itself to the structure, the organization, the militancy.*

We live in a plural society and we are called to bear witness
to the faith in this society, not in another one. As Pope Francis
said, "We are no longer in that time. It's over. We are no longer
in Christianity, no more. Today we are no longer the only ones
who produce culture, nor the first, nor the most listened to."[28]
In fact, the fundamental value of current society is freedom,
and the various cultural voices demand an equal right to express themselves in the public space. What does this mean for
our presence in society as Christians? What type of presence is
requested of us Christians in this plural context? In order to be
a presence, we have no need of strength, power, or hegemony.
In fact, Christianity is communicated through the splendour
of a personal or community testimony that documents the
newness of life that is born of the faith.

But this leads to a whole other chapter that I consider crucial, above all in these times, namely, the relationship between
freedom and truth. This is one of the points I most tried to deal
with in *Disarming Beauty*. The Church has made a very long
journey to arrive at the self-awareness now expressed in the
Vatican II text *Dignitatis Humanae*, which affirms that the truth
cannot be imposed, unless it is by the power of the truth
itself.[29] This means that even if the Church acknowledges the
truth of the event of Christ, this truth can never be imposed.
Nobody can be forced to believe. Faith can only be witnessed
to, and the other person can recognize the event of Christ
incarnate in the existence of people who live everything starting from the faith. But, as Giussani stressed forcefully at the
beginning of our movement, this recognition can only happen
through freedom. He was perfectly aware that the recognition
of and adherence to the Christian fact cannot be the result of
any human project but are a grace that passes through freedom. "Our immediate ... characteristic was the accent placed
on the value of freedom."[30] For this reason, as I already said,
when he was speaking about student associations he insisted
that if a school had only one non-Catholic student, the associ-

ation would have to be inspired by human values acceptable to that student too, respecting and embracing his or her position.

Even just one non-Catholic ...

Yes, even just one. From this point of view, I believe we have to return to the *Dignitatis Humanae* document of the Second Vatican Council on religious freedom, and also Benedict XVI's reflection on it in his famous speech to the Roman Curia in December 2005. Some thought that the document on religious freedom interrupted the Catholic tradition, marking a break with the traditional teaching of the Church. In reality, as often happens in the life of the Church, what was broken was not tradition but simply a certain interpretation or a certain way of living Christianity that had ended up losing touch with the origin. With the declaration on religious freedom, the Church was not saying something like "Since we have been unable to convince people that Christianity is the truth, and the conditions today are far more difficult than they were before, we accept religious freedom." No! That document was the outcome of a journey, a deepened look at the nature of Christianity, matured in relation to the provocations of history, which led to the reaffirmation of what characterized the beginnings of Christianity and belonged to the original patrimony of the Church, that is, that the truth, which is Christ, needs nothing else to communicate itself than the splendour and attraction of the truth itself. Thus we were freed from any kind of temptation to hegemony and we were brought back to the origin.

For this reason, the situation in which we find ourselves now is an extraordinary opportunity for us Christians to rediscover the nature of Christianity. Faith by its very nature cannot be imposed from outside. It calls upon the freedom of women and men and therefore, as Pope Benedict XVI said, every generation must regain it anew. Even more so in a society that makes freedom its cipher, the truth can be affirmed only if it becomes personal conviction, that is, if each person gives it free acknowledgment. In the final analysis, the only power that Christianity can use to assert itself publicly is its interior

truth. The power of numbers, of means, of structures or marketing strategies serves nothing. Everything happens through
the power of truth, through the attraction it exerts. We see this
in the saints, women and men whose lives radiated the beauty
of Christianity, who changed the existence of many people and
thus also history. This is the testimony to which we are called,
both in personal acts and in communitarian ones. There is no
other way of communicating the truth outside this, because of
the very nature of truth itself. In fact, truth has become an
event of life, has made itself visible in the life of a man: this is
the Christian announcement, which is renewed in the same
terms today through those who have been bowled over by the
fact of Christ.

*Pope Benedict XVI, in a conversation about his trip to Cuba with
Cardinal Ortega y Alamina, said, "The Church is not in the world
to change governments"*[31] *and also said that dialogue is the only
possible way. What do you think this means, and what keys for
understanding does this gaze offer the life of a movement like CL?*

Christ did not come to bring the world one of the possible
fronts, one of the possible political options. He put on the
table of history the greatest promise that humanity has ever
received: those who follow Him will have the hundred-fold
here below, an intensity a hundred times greater in every
aspect of life, and then will experience eternal life. Christ
claims to be the answer to every single person's boundless
desire for happiness. But this is also the one interesting
announcement for real women and men. The challenge today
is not merely to change a government. The true challenge is
the nihilism that is gripping the young and the less young, that
is, the belief that deep down, there is no adequate answer to
your own desire. In the hustle and bustle of daily life you think
you can manage, but when life presses urgently, you become
aware of the sense of destruction that dwells in it, of all the lack
of hope. Can a change of structures or governments respond to
this? Here you can grasp the import of Christianity and the
contribution that Christians, according to how well they live

what they have received, can offer people. Recently a non-believer journalist told me, "You have no idea what you bring!"

This reminds me of a speech Ratzinger gave before becoming pope, a concept that he then repeated during a meeting with journalists on the flight to Prague, the most de-Christianized European capital. He said that non-believers need believers to prompt in them questions about the fact that an afterworld can exist, that truth can exist. Non-believers need believers in order to be uneasy. But at the same time and in the same way, believers need non-believers, their doubt, their questions, in order to avoid transforming their faith into an ideology. If you always need to enter into dialogue, into contact, with those who harbour doubts, with those who challenge you, with those who ask you existential questions, you are always forced to question yourself. You are forced not to take your faith for granted and at the same time, to welcome and make your own that question, that existential wound, which you certainly cannot answer with ready-made answers or ultra-abridged doctrine summaries.

This is the beauty of plural society: this constant opportunity for exchange, so that you find yourself with people who ask you questions that you cannot answer by cheating. In trying to respond, you become aware of your reasons for believing. Dialogue with those who do not believe gives us the opportunity to become more conscious of what we have received, and makes it more difficult for us to transform it into a framework or ideology. With their questions, they help us not reduce what has happened to us to something acquired, a possession. Christ is not something we have conquered. We are the ones who, by grace, without any merit, have been attracted by Him. We are the ones who, by grace, belong to Him. For this reason, we feel humanly close to and share all the anguish of those who do not believe, those who have not had the gift of faith, those who are searching, those who ask.

The doubt of the other person, the doubt of those who do not believe, nonetheless remains an open wound; it questions me.

Certainly, because the others, with their doubts and questions, call me to live faith not as a point of arrival, but as a wound that is never healed, making me the travelling companion of anyone I find on the road. Contrary to what is often thought, finding never extinguishes the search, but fans the flame. I will never forget the words of Hans Urs von Balthasar, "Just as the swimmer, even when he has acquired increasing mastery of his art, must *always* swim in order to avoid drowning, the lover must live every day anew at the very origin of love and therein continue to probe and question it. In the same way, the knower must daily ask anew what truth is, although, to repeat, this question is not the same as fruitless and destructive doubt."[32] You cannot stay afloat without swimming. Therefore, faith is not a question resolved once and for all, thanks be to God. I want to be able to say *yes* to Christ every morning, not mechanically, and not just for the sake of saying it. I want this *yes* to become more and more mine each time, just as a man would desire to be able to say to his wife every day, "I love you now," but not out of habit, because this would make everything become formal. Faith has this vivacity. The problem arises when, instead of becoming increasingly alive, faith becomes increasingly formal and mechanical, and thus slowly dies out; if you do not live it as love, if you do not realize ever anew what a grace encountering Christ has been for you, you become sterile. In the same way, if a man does not realize what a grace it is to have met the beloved, if he does not desire to tell her now that he loves her and to feel he is loved by her, everything is reduced to habit and the drive to know her and deepen the relationship with her slackens.

Never take anything for granted, never! Only in this way can we "support people in their search as fellow-seekers, and at the same time ... also give them the certainty that God has found us and, consequently, that we can find Him."[33] I had the fortune recently to have a fascinating conversation with a person in rationalist doubt, and I was amazed that he wanted to end our dialogue with a provocation to Christians to "come out of the closet," because, he said, even though not everyone has their faith, everyone needs their light.

In the 1950s, Fr Giussani was impatient with certain schematic rules in effect in the associations of the time, such as Catholic Action. For example, there was a rigid division between men and women. How did and how does CL live the Second Vatican Council?

In his speech opening the Council, John XXIII said that the Christian announcement had to reach "the numerous fields of human activity that touch individuals, families, and social life,"[34] to make itself present precisely there, where a dramatic fracture between faith and life was happening. The Council's concern coincided with what Giussani and other personalities of the Church had begun to sense in the 1950s, namely, a reduction of Christianity on the one hand to the formalism of certain habits and on the other hand to a package of truths to which one simply needed to assent. The result was a dualism between faith and life and a progressive distancing from the Christian experience. The first great help that the Council provided in this regard, as I have already observed, was the constitution *Dei Verbum*, because of the way it conceived of Revelation as not only words but words and actions intrinsically and intimately bound. Thus Revelation is an event, as the fact of Jesus demonstrates, and as the Old Testament had already demonstrated. Jesus communicated His identity not only when He spoke but also when He acted, when He looked at Zacchaeus, when He entered his home; with His way of being, He introduced into the social and cultural reality of His time a newness without compare. When the people saw Him act they could not help but be amazed: "Never have we seen anything of the kind!"

Giussani went to teach at the Berchet high school because of his profound awareness of Christianity as an event that transforms people's lives. He realized that many young people no longer perceived Christianity in these terms. Cardinal Ratzinger grasped Fr Giussani's intuition very well when he said in his funeral homily that for Giussani, "Christianity is not an intellectual system, a collection of dogmas, or moralism. Christianity is instead an encounter, a love story; it is an event,"[35] from which friendship, culture, and new action arise. The Council marked an awareness of what the Scriptures say; it was a way to return to the origin and showed everyone that Christianity is communicated as an attraction. If only the words of Christianity were left, it could not be adequate to the expectancy of the heart.

A second great intuition of the Council concerned the communitarian aspect of the faith. Giussani remembered how the Student Youth celebrated the publication of the constitution *Lumen Gentium*, which so magnificently placed emphasis on the Church as a community that can be seen, experienced, and encountered. *Lumen Gentium* begins with these lines, "Christ is the light of nations. Because this is so, this Sacred Synod gathered together in the Holy Spirit eagerly desires, by proclaiming the Gospel to every creature (Mark 16:15), to bring the light of Christ to all men, a light brightly visible on the countenance of the Church." Commenting, Giussani said, "It is in the face of the Church that His face tracks me down in my wanderings, in my roaming around, and fills me with Himself, stops me as I make a mistaken step, calls out to me, and upholds me."[36]

Finally, a third great intuition is contained in the constitution *Gaudium et Spes* which Giussani appreciated from the very beginning because it shows interest in and passion for the world, esteem for human efforts, notwithstanding the perception of their ultimate sadness because of the incompleteness they suffer. In the famous Section 22 of that document it says, "Christ, the final Adam, by the revelation of the mystery of the Father and His love, fully reveals man to man himself." John Paul II would take this up again in his encyclical *Redemptor Hominis*. It is in the encounter with Christ that man is revealed to man.

If you compared the texts and documents of Student Youth guided by Fr Giussani with the texts of the Council, many analogies, in addition to those already summarized and highlighted, would jump out at you. For this reason, Giussani said, "So, we lived the time of the council without any celebratory language but with great hope and as an authoritative confirmation of certain intuitions that were already taking shape within our own experience."[37]

What is CL's stance regarding traditionalism?

The question is connected to what I have just tried to say, because traditionalism has not perceived the deepened understanding of revelation that the Church reached and expressed in *Dei Verbum*, which I mentioned just before; it stops at a purely intellectual conception of religion. For Fr Giussani, Christianity is only an event. Here you see his distance from all forms of traditionalism; they have nothing in common, not simply regarding the secondary expressions, in the consequences, but concerning the original core of the conception of our movement, which John Paul II would also recognize in his 2002 letter to Fr Giussani, by then near the end of his life, in which he affirmed that "Christianity, even before being a sum of doctrines or a rule for salvation, is thus the 'event' of an encounter. This is the insight and experience that you have transmitted in these years to so many persons who have adhered to the Communion and Liberation movement."[38] For Giussani, Christianity is an event that has the form of an encounter – as the Gospel documents, beginning with the encounters of the disciples – and therefore it is something you can experience. Here is another great difference from traditionalism.

Traditionalists consider the word "experience" to be smoke and mirrors.

They consider the word "experience" very risky because they conceive of it in a very reductive way, as the road that leads to subjectivism and sentimentalism. Thanks be to God, Fr Giussani had to respond to a request for clarification on this theme from then-Cardinal Montini, because of the accusations made against Student Youth in the beginning. Some thought that his insistence on experience endangered the objective communication of the faith. Giussani answered the Cardinal with a brief and dense text in which he clarified the meaning of the word "experience" and affirmed the exact opposite: the thing that could make the objective content of the faith interesting and accessi-

ble was precisely the experience of it. By that time, the words of
Christianity had become abstract and empty for most young
people. Only experience could fill them anew with meaning.
Now, for traditionalists, the nexus with experience is an unac-
ceptable risk, while for Giussani, it was the one possibility.

In order to be Christian today it is necessary to discover
within your own experience the pertinence of Christianity to
the needs of life; you have to discover that it is worthwhile to
be Christian. I would add that Giussani never accepted a
reduced concept of experience. He did not reduce experience
in the immanentistic, subjectivistic, and sentimental sense. He
forcefully stressed that every proposal should be evaluated in
terms of the heart's needs, and in this he was profoundly modern, but these needs are an objective and "infallible" criterion,
or in other words, an original structure with which everyone
is endowed that enables the recognition of the truth. Therefore, the true is that which proves to correspond with the
structural and ineradicable needs of our being. As Ratzinger
said, "We can recognize only that which finds a correspondence in us."[39] In that first encounter, why did John and
Andrew immediately recognize who Jesus was, not thorough-
ly and in detail, but in His divine value, in His being something exceptional? They did so because they had an unrivalled
experience of correspondence between that presence and the
expectations of their hearts. This is how we can grasp the truth
of Christianity. It is like when you encounter a person and you
say, "He's the one," or "She's the one," because you have a certain experience of correspondence.

The Christian encounter follows the same dynamic; in fact,
it fulfills this dynamic. The disciples encountered someone
who responded like no other to the needs of their hearts, and
they recognized it. There is nothing subjective or sentimental
in this. If someone should think so, and theorize the need for
a confirmation outside experience itself, they would need to
ask themselves, drawing upon something I mentioned before,
what John and Andrew would have done if they had not found

in their own experience the correspondence with the person in front of them. To whom could they have gone to find out whether He was or was not the long-awaited Messiah? Nobody could have given them a supplement of certainty that they had not received from experience. A mistaken conception of experience leads people to question this approach and thus, likewise, to conceive of tradition in a rigid way. I remember how Giussani answered a question on traditionalism: "It's one thing to affirm Tradition as 'forms,' and it's another thing to bring it forward as contents of value."[40]

In any case, the great rule is this: tradition cannot subsist except according to an expressive newness, evoked by the Eternal Father through the circumstances in which the Church finds itself. Tradition is not tradition if it does not renew itself. This is the opposite of the idea that anything new casts doubt on tradition. No, precisely this renewal has enabled the Church to face all the historic vicissitudes, communicating in an ever-new way the nature of faith, which is always the same. Imagine the Benedictines after the barbarian invasions, Saint Francis at the height of the Middle Ages, Saint Ignatius of Loyola and many others after the Protestant Reformation. In every age, the effort to respond to the challenges of the present has been an opportunity to understand the faith more deeply. This has enabled the faith to continue to be itself. Just remember the great journey the Church has made to comprehend the very nature of Christ, in the councils of the fourth century, discussing what could be included in the Creed. The form had to evolve constantly in order to conserve the fundamental core of the faith received; in order to save it, it had to be said in a different way. This is what at times is not understood. In order to *tradere*, that is, in order for there to be communication, transmission of the tradition, it must renew itself. The Church has done this for 2,000 years, embracing and transmitting "the living voice of the Gospel"[41] that the Holy Spirit caused to resound in it. For this reason, I do not know where the traditionalist idea can come from: it goes against what the Church and the Scriptures say.

The very Spirit who nurtures the living tradition is the one of whom we spoke regarding the charisms. Jesus said, "But when He comes, the Spirit of truth, He will guide you to all truth."[42] The Church gains ever-deeper awareness of itself over time, precisely through its own life, thanks to the light and energy of the Spirit who dwells in it. A man as intelligent as Newman wrote a book on the development of dogma, showing that there is no true continuity without development.[43]

What about traditionalism in the liturgical field?

Giussani always lived the liturgy with attention to the essential, precisely because of the nature of what happens in the celebration. In order for it to be ever more limpid and beautiful, he took care with the choice of songs and the soberness of the gestures, without adding anything out of the ordinary to make it more attractive. He educated people to live the liturgy as the relationship with Christ present in the sacrament. He needed no extra ornamentation to make it more "digestible." Everything necessary was already present in the liturgical gesture. Through all that he did, he wanted to show that the liturgy is part of the communication of the faith.

5

In the Company of the Popes

The CL Movement and Authority in the Church

Can you describe the relationship between the Communion and Liberation movement and John Paul II?

CL knew John Paul II before he became pope, because of the relationship that the movement, through various groups of people, had cultivated with Catholics in some countries behind what was then called the Iron Curtain. Fr Francesco Ricci met Archbishop of Cracow Karol Wojtyła in the second half of the 1960s. Fr Giussani met him in Poland in 1973 and in Rome in January 1979, a few months after his election. Right away, Fr Giussani wrote to the whole movement, "My friends, let us serve this man, let us serve Christ in this great man with all our existence."[1] A great opportunity for deepening the relationship with the pope was the encyclical *Redemptor Hominis*, which was truly a milestone in our journey. Fr Giussani had a special edition printed and had the whole movement study it for a full year, because it describes the nature of Christianity and the Church. The first line of the encyclical, "The redeemer of man, Jesus Christ, is the centre of the universe and of history," became a sort of manifesto. The relationship with the pope grew increasingly closer.

Several times, young people of the movement went to the Vatican to greet him, invited by John Paul II himself for the occasion of what he called his "monthly birthday." In 1982 he went to the Meeting of Rimini and invited listeners to build the civilization of truth and love. In 1984 he received the move-

ment in an audience for the thirtieth anniversary of its foundation and on that occasion gave CL its missionary mandate:
"Go into all the world to bring the truth, the beauty, and the
peace which are found in Christ the Redeemer."[2] Fr Giussani's
response was immediate: "We have to empty the boot. We have
to turn Italy upside down and dump everyone out to go out
into all the world."[3] From then on, many bishops on their
return from their *ad limina* visits to Rome began to ask to have
members of the movement come to live in their diocese, and
thus many priests made themselves available to go on mis-
sions, and university students or adults decided to accept
opportunities to study or work abroad. In this way, the movement's spread had a great new impetus.

I would say that at the origin of all this, there was the deep
understanding between the pope and Fr Giussani, an attune-
ment that continued until the end. In one of their first meetings, in January 1980, the pope said, "Your way of facing problems is similar to mine or, better, it is the same."[4]

*What is the relationship between the movement and the bishops
who, especially during the pontificate of Pope Jean Paul II, were chosen from among the priests of CL?*

When a member of the movement became a bishop (or
took on responsibilities in politics and thus acquired a public
role), Fr Giussani's choice was to free him from any worries
about responsibility in the movement, so that he could put all
his intelligence, all his affection, and all of himself at the service of the new mission. From the moment of his nomination
as bishop, a priest of CL therefore only had to answer to what
the Church asked of him. Giussani always sought to generate
adults willing to take on responsibility at every level, including
the ecclesiastical one. Respecting the distinctions between
roles, he maintained personal friendships, with reciprocal
esteem and freedom, with those involved in such responsibilities. Following his example, I have sought to do the same.

*What was the relationship between CL and Cardinal Carlo
Maria Martini, archbishop of Milan between 1980 and 2002? It
has been said that relations were not always easy.*

Fr Giussani always spoke of Cardinal Martini's paternal attitude in embracing and accepting the movement in his diocese. He was profoundly grateful, for example, when the archbishop gave him permission to set up a chapel in the movement's Milan headquarters for the celebration of daily Mass. From the moment of his arrival, the archbishop showed attention to Fr Giussani. In 1988 he invited him to speak together with Oscar Luigi Scalfaro on the occasion of the great pilgrimage of young people of the Caravaggio diocese. Right away it was evident that they shared a conviction about what the new evangelization should be: not new techniques or a strategy, but communicating enthusiasm at being Christian. Martini had great esteem for Fr Giussani in his emphasis on the fact of the Incarnation. In 1995, during a meeting of Ambrosian priests, he thanked the Lord for having given Giussani "his gift of being able to constantly reexpress the core of Christianity. You always, every time you speak, go back to this core, which is the Incarnation and in a thousand different ways, you repropose it again and again."[5]

Fr Giussani appreciated Martini's constant concern for peace and above all his emphasis on the value of ecumenism, understood as the capacity to enter into a relationship with everyone, with that attention – visible in the cardinal – to capture every crumb of truth to be found in anyone, even those furthest away. I think of Martini's "Chair for Non-believers," a lecture series in which he dialogued with people of the most diverse orientations. Giussani identified deeply with this ecumenism. Another aspect that struck him was the idea of charity as the sharing of needs. In this, too, they agreed. I read about a very large conference at the Milan Palalido arena in 1990; there were thousands of people engaged in works of charity, with Fr Giussani sitting at the table next to the archbishop, who said he was amazed at the "sea of charity"[6] in front of him. On other issues they had differences, for example, on how to understand the relationships between charism and institution, movement and parish, but always in communion, as far as I know.

*What was the relationship between the movement and Benedict
XVI, who has lived for many years, and still lives, with the care and
collaboration of some women of the* Memores Domini, *that is, lay-
women who have chosen to live as virgins according to the charism
of Fr Giussani?*

The strong relationship between Fr Giussani and Cardinal
Ratzinger is well known. Giussani cared a great deal about the
dialogues with him, as he held him in great regard, prizing his
theological intelligence and the solidity of his faith. They had
a number of meetings, during which Giussani took the opportunity to submit for the cardinal's evaluation some of his intuitions and formulations that he wanted to feel entirely peaceful about, for example, as he himself related, "Mystery and sign
coincide" or "If the word was made flesh, it is in flesh that we
find Him, identically," or existentially, "The charism comes
before dogma," and so on.[7] He referred enthusiastically to their
deep consonance. So yes, they shared a special closeness.

In the beginning of 2013, as pope, Ratzinger spoke of Giussani in these terms: "I became acquainted with his faith, his
joy, his strength, the wealth of his ideas, and the creativity of
his faith. So it was that a true friendship developed."[8] But the
cardinal's most important and profound act was coming to
celebrate the funeral of Giussani, at the invitation of John Paul
II. This gesture of friendship expressed all his recognition of
the value of the relationship they had shared.

*What was and is your personal relationship with Pope Benedict
XVI?*

Apart from a few occasional greetings, I have had only one
opportunity for a meeting with him, when I became the leader
of the movement. I can say that our relationship is infused
with Ratzinger's esteem for Fr Giussani. Right away, he made
me feel part of their friendship, which continued through the
bond with my poor person. Later I had the good fortune to
speak with him several times for clarification on some things
– as Giussani did – to ask for his advice on some choices I had
to make, and I have always been welcomed with surprising
esteem and familiarity. I was very struck by his decision to step

back from the pontificate; it was a most extraordinary fact, the confirmation of his freedom regarding any role. The certainty he had in Christ, and to which he always bore witness, enabled him to take a step of this kind.

I enjoy rereading him often: he is crystal clear in his way of addressing problems and expresses himself with surprising simplicity even when he is dealing with complex topics. So there is not only the personal companionship, but also the deep companionship that is his magisterium, the wealth of the work he has produced for the life of all the Church and all of us.

During the first Vatileaks, a letter you wrote to Pope Benedict XVI about the succession of the Diocese of Milan was published in a newspaper and then in a book. It was part of a series of private consultations that the apostolic nunciature in Italy normally conducts in these cases. Your letter not only contained your favorable opinion about the nomination of then patriarch of Venice Angelo Scola to head the Ambrosian Archdiocese but also contained negative judgments on Cardinals Martini and Tettamanzi. Given that this letter was certainly not intended to become public, are you sorry that you wrote it? Did it contain your personal judgments or was it the fruit of the work of the movement's leaders' group?

In fact, my letter was confidential, a *voto sub secreto* that the apostolic nuncio in Italy explicitly requested of me. In the letter I expressed some observations on the diocese of Milan, gathered during conversations with some leaders of the movement that took place in previous years. I never would have wanted to give scandal. What most pained me was the way the letter was interpreted, perceived, and presented as a direct accusation of Cardinals Martini and Tettamanzi, which corresponded neither to the intention nor to the meaning of my words.

It is true that over the years there have been misunderstandings, certainly also due to our fault, but the central content of that letter was an analysis and a judgment on a state of things that involved all of us: from the very first words, I wrote that as Christians we shared the responsibility for having accepted the fracture characteristic of modernity between faith and life, to the detriment of the cohesiveness of the Christian experience, reduced to intimism and moralism, and of its power for credible testimony in society. The rest was an attempt, without a doubt approximate and perhaps also awkward, to highlight some symptoms of the change of era that did not concern individual persons and that now is clear to everyone.

Even though I did not live in Milan before 2004, I also felt involved, so much so that when Cardinal Martini died, I wrote in *Corriere della Sera* that Fr Giussani always spoke of the paternal attitude of the archbishop, who had embraced and accepted a reality like CL in the diocese of Milan. I also said, "It pains and saddens us if we did not always find the most adequate way to collaborate with his arduous mission and if we have given a pretext for equivocal interpretations of our relationship with him, starting with myself." I concluded by saying, "It is my hope that we never tire of searching for that collaboration which is indispensable – especially today – to the mission of the Church."[9] Years before, Martini himself had encouraged that, saying, "The novelty of the so-called new evangelization should not be sought in new techniques of announcement, but first of all in the rediscovered enthusiasm of feeling ourselves believers and in trust in the action of the Holy Spirit,"[10] so as to "evangelize contagiously ... from person to person."[11]

Those considerations have led the way for the work of these years: in line with these indications, there have been an increasing number of opportunities for encounter, collaboration, and reciprocal testimony with the different realities of the diocese, from Catholic Action to the other movements, and with the offices of the Curia, especially those dedicated to the laity, youth, and work, for example, the work with prisoners, the first document co-signed by all the Catholic associations on the upcoming administrative elections, and some shared cultural initiatives. Then there are many people in the movement involved in parish councils, catechism, parish youth centres, and a myriad of works of charity, people who collaborate in the renewal of the life of the Ambrosian Church, for a "Milan Church of the People" able to make Pope Francis feel at home, as he himself said in the Angelus on the Sunday after his visit to the city.[12]

A lot of controversy surrounded Pope Benedict XVI's decision to give up the papacy. Some have written that Ratzinger was in some way forced to leave because of a plot organized to harm him. From what you know of the pope emeritus, do you think he might have stepped down because he was pressured to do so?

I certainly do not. It seems to me that he acted with such amazing freedom that no explanation of this type can account for what we saw. I am speaking about what I believe struck everyone: a person at the height of his "power" who decides to step down, with full awareness and profound peace. Being able to do this demands a fullness of life that makes a person free. As Benedict XVI himself explained in his book interview with Peter Seewald, *Last Testament: In His Own Words*, he always conceived of his ministry as service, and his act of stepping down began in a dialogue of faith with the Lord, from the clear awareness of how crucial that service is, and from a superabundance that made him free. I would add that giving credence to conjectures about plots means going against the pope emeritus's own statements. All the interpretations of that type clash with what Benedict XVI himself said and with the free act of his stepping down, with all that it says to us.

What was your reaction in March 2013 when Cardinal Jorge Mario Bergoglio was elected as the successor of Benedict XVI?

I was very surprised. I knew that as a cardinal he had shown interest in the figure of Fr Giussani and had always accepted invitations from some members of the movement in Argentina to present the books of our founder. Also, his friendship with people of the Rome community were known to me. Once I began to see him in action, it became evident to me – beyond what might at first sight seem to indicate a break from Benedict XVI, so different are they in temperament and history – that the whole magisterium of

Francis is a radicalization of that of Benedict XVI. Francis has brought to completion a series of Pope Benedict XIV's intuitions, and because of the way he relates, he has made them accessible to everyone.

Pope Francis desires to respond to the new situation that has come about, in his words, a "change of epoch." Simple people understand his message very well. His way of being present, his actions and words immediately touch the needs and wounds of contemporary people. This capacity to tune in to people, to dialogue with their wounded hearts, also characterizes the soul of Benedict, but Pope Francis's pastoral nature, temperament, and personality of faith enable him to testify to the face of mercy with a simplicity, immediacy, and an embrace of the other that forcefully reaches people who are at once the most different and the most simple. Pope Francis is a grace for the Church in the world today. The one question is whether we accept the provocation of his witness, in order to learn from his way of being how to be a witness like him. It is evident that a man cannot do everything or go everywhere, and so he chooses to do things like going Lampedusa or Lesbos, in doing so showing us that it is necessary to go out, that it is necessary to embrace the other, witnessing to the faith with the same acts as Jesus.

In order for this to become ours, the inheritance of everyone, the Church, that is, all of us, need to follow the testimony of the pope, imitating it and understanding the consequences in our life. So allow me to say let's be open to being struck and provoked by him!

Among the criticisms of the current papacy, some of them decidedly strong and sometimes even disdainful, others gentler, many come from journalists, priests, and historic exponents of the Communion and Liberation movement. Why do you think this is? Are they tied to an interpretation of Fr Giussani's thought?

I must admit that the reasons for such positions elude me, and I sincerely do not understand them. However, I want to clarify that those statements and criticisms do not in any way represent the position of CL. We find ourselves facing a change of epoch, as Pope Francis defines it, and if you do not grasp this you will not be able to understand his way of acting. It is impossible to respond to the current challenges in the same ways that people faced challenges in past epochs. In order to open up to new ways, you have to realize the situation we are in, and for this, you need a certain willingness to let the things that happen make you question yourself.

I truly cannot understand certain positions against the pope, from every point of view. They have nothing to do with the attitude that Giussani showed us in his relationship with the popes, with the consciousness he communicated to us about the figure and function of the pope in the life of the Church. There are scores of texts in which he speaks of this, but I will limit myself to quoting one: "The face of that man [Christ] is today the whole set of believers, who are the sign of it in the world, or – as Saint Paul said – are the Body, the mystical Body, called also 'people of God,' guided as a guarantee by a living person, the bishop of Rome."[13] I can comprehend that people may not understand some aspects of the pontificate and dissent from this or that initiative. But that this dissent should be made public, that it should be expressed daily, at times disrespectfully, inviting people to have a negative attitude toward the successor of Peter, I consider harmful to the life of the Church.

Pope Francis's March 2015 speech in Saint Peter's Square was considered by many to be a "scolding" of CL, although some of the references, such as not preserving the charism in a bottle and leaving behind self-referentiality, belong to his current magisterium and have been addressed to other movements and religious orders as well. Why? How did you receive that speech?

We did not go to Rome out of formalism or to celebrate an anniversary but with a precise question, that of anyone who belongs to the life of the movement. How can the freshness of the charism be maintained? How can the origin be kept alive? How can we avoid the crystallization of the grace received, its transformation into something already known, into a reality that only refers to the past? We went to the pope with this desire, with this question in our hearts. And Francis answered us in a tremendous way, first of all by making the freshness of the charism happen right there in Saint Peter's Square. With his gaze, he made us perceive how Christ is at the centre of life. This truly amazed us. When you are looked at with truth, when you hear and see a witness who says there is only one at the centre, Christ, you realize more fully that this is the only thing you need. This is what Fr Giussani always tried to do, to enable us to start anew in every situation, overcoming all formalism and tiredness. All the rest is a consequence of this fact, of the experience we had that day, when the gaze of Christ happened in our life again. It seems to me that the call not to be closed in on ourselves, not to be self-referential, is something that concerns every Christian and every ecclesial experience, so much so that the pope has repeated it, and continues to repeat it to everyone. Only by remaining bound to Jesus, only by allowing ourselves to be encountered by Him, can we avoid succumbing to the danger of self-referentiality.

The 7 March audience was a stunning experience that we will never forget, as memory and as constant call to live the authenticity of the charism. Francis spoke so openly to us that we were entirely his. He referred to Giussani's words about the encounter and the relationship with Christ, emphasizing points that are dear to us, such as John and Andrew's encounter with Jesus, or the calling of Matthew. This is what happened in Saint Peter's Square, and all the rest flowed from there, including the attitude that he asked us to take on, drawing upon the words of Fr Giussani: "Never in history is Christianity realized as a fixity of positions to defend, which relates to the new as pure antithesis; Christianity is the principle of redemption, which takes on the new, preserving it."[14] The pope urged us to seek out the glimmer of truth present in everyone we encounter on our road – which is the opposite of self-referentiality – and to valorize

every crumb of good that we can find in others, as he himself shows us. Only through the superabundance experienced in the relationship with Christ can we be so totally
open, 360 degrees, to the aspect of the good and the beautiful that exists in everyone.

To your mind, what is the heart of the message in the exhortation
Evangelii gaudium, *considered from the very beginning the road*
map of the pontificate, and which the pope himself recently defined
as his true programmatic document? Do you think the Church has
focused on this? Has the CL movement?

The entire message is contained in the title and the first sentence: "The joy of the gospel fills the hearts and lives of all
who encounter Jesus ... With Christ joy is constantly born
anew."[15] It is like his "dominant thought," to use Leopardi's
expression. What predominates in him, to put it briefly? In
those who have met Christ, the thing that prevails as a feeling
about oneself, as an attitude that regards everything, is joy, a
happiness that fills life. This is what happened to those who
met Jesus, as we read in the Gospel stories. Joy is the reverberation of the newness introduced by Christ, of the newness
that is Christ Himself; His presence fills life and makes it glad.
The intensity of living generated by the encounter with Christ
is the hundred-fold here below, the experience of the fulfillment that people desire, but do not know how to reach, and
that is pure gift, pure grace. Therefore Francis says, "I never tire
of repeating those words of Benedict XVI" – here is a sign of
the profound continuity between the two pontificates –
"which take us to the very heart of the Gospel: 'Being a Christian is not the result of an ethical choice or a lofty idea, but the
encounter with an event, a person, which gives life a new horizon and a decisive direction.'"[16] It is interesting to note that
Pope Francis's first document, the road map of his pontificate,
contains practically at the beginning a reference to Benedict
XVI's first encyclical, *Deus caritas est.*

The pope tells us that in this event, in the encounter with
Christ, there is already everything. The rest is a development
of this fact. From there flows all the rest that *Evangelii gaudi-*

um develops. Francis stresses that Christianity is not communicated through proselytism but "by attraction" (another
expression drawn from Benedict XVI, in his homily at Aparecida), and therefore, "pastoral ministry in a missionary style is
not obsessed with the disjointed transmission of a multitude
of doctrines to be insistently imposed." Christianity is an event
that attracts life and fills it with joy. Thus the proposal is sim-
plified, as if in a time of great confusion and bewilderment the
pope wanted to redirect attention to the core, the essence of
the Gospel. "The heart of its message will always be the same:
the God who revealed His immense love in the crucified and
risen Christ."[17] This is what Francis wants to communicate in
the whole document, even when he goes into the details, the
particulars. The core from which everything else is born and
develops is the event of Christ, the joy that flows from it, as
expressed in the title.

That title is already a program. The pope cares deeply about
announcing this event to every woman and man. We see it in
every action he takes, wherever he goes. In every encounter, in
every moment of his life, through his embrace, through his
closeness, he wants to communicate the embrace of Christ,
what has happened to him in the encounter with Christ, the
joy that fills him in any situation, before any person. The concept of mission that Francis develops in *Evangelii gaudium*
flows from this. "It would be wrong to see it as a heroic individual undertaking, for it is first and foremost the Lord's work
… Jesus is 'the first and greatest evangelizer.'"[18] The true newness is the one that He Himself mysteriously wants to generate. It is not the outcome of a strategy or organic system of doctrine, nor is it a project worked out at a conference table; it is
simply the communication, the testimony of what has happened. Francis draws upon the magisterium of previous popes
on this point, when he says, for example, with Paul VI, that
"modern man listens more willingly to witnesses than to
teachers"[19] or, in other words, is more sensitive to experience
than to doctrine, more to life and facts than to theories. If you
look attentively, you will see, just as we have already said many

times, that precisely this is the concept of revelation contained in the constitution *Dei Verbum*: Christianity is not a set of doctrines, but an event, facts and words that are intimately connected. Through *Evangelii gaudium* the pope calls the whole Church to this, as a full realization of the Second Vatican Council.

Do you think this has been focused on and understood in the movement and in the Church?

For us, this was the core that we recognized as soon as we read the document. I am not able to comment on what has happened in the whole Church. I think that a document like this requires time, because it expresses and proposes an approach that is not assimilated from one day to the other. But the magisterium of Pope Francis has already begun to have an impact as a new gaze that is reaching people, a gaze full of tenderness and mercy, such that many people are drawing close to the Church for the first time, and others are reopening a file they thought they had closed long ago. There are signs, maybe initial ones, of something that is beginning to make headway, and that I think is a point of no return for the years ahead.

What is the main message of the exhortation Amoris laetitia *on marriage and the family?*

It seems to me that its message flows from the same source, that is, the Christian event that generates an experience of joy. This is the source of the pope's tender and merciful gaze on families, on the concrete reality of the married; it is like he is applying *Evangelii gaudium* to family life. *Amoris laetitia* expresses that gaze of Jesus documented in the Gospel: "His heart was moved with pity for them, for they were like sheep without a shepherd,"[20] that is, they were disturbed, disoriented, trapped in their own difficulties, caught in the gears of their own lives. With this gaze born of the faith, the pope wants to draw close to the concrete reality of families, to bring to their struggles as well the newness that is the encounter with Christ. He is not interested in mere rhetoric denouncing current evils. Above all, what matters to him is that people, especially youth, can encounter witnesses who will make them understand the reasons for choosing the married life, witnesses who show those in love, those who live such a beautiful experience as falling in love, that marriage is the great promise that the beauty of that moment can last and mature, without the relationship growing old, becoming formal, and changing into a cage. This problem concerns everyone, Christians and non-Christians. As he explains in the apostolic exhortation, it is not solved merely by insisting on doctrinal issues or moral calls. First, the existential situation must be faced, starting from a person's desire to love the other forever. But falling in love is not enough to support the relationship or make it last; it is the beginning of the journey. Marriage is not the photograph of a moment, but a dynamic journey of growth and realization.

The pope's whole effort is focused on how to accompany, support, and constantly reawaken that beginning, so that love does not grow old. Nothing is more fascinating than encountering the beloved. And yet, even so, often the "you" that was so crucial in the beginning can become distant, almost a stranger, and be perceived as an obstacle to self-fulfillment. At times these things scandalize us. But when Jesus talked about the duration of love, the disciples saw the difficulty of the goal right away, and their powerlessness to achieve it, and said, "Well, it's better not to marry at all, then!"[21] If Christianity is not offered as a fact that accompanies life and enables people to face this difficulty as well, they will end up thinking like the disciples that "It's better not to get married," as if marriage was the tomb of love. Jesus brought to the concrete situation of families the greatest promise that can be made to a couple, to two people who fall in love, namely, the fulfillment of the desire for duration that belongs to the beginning of every true relationship, the fullness of the beauty contained in falling in love. If we let Christ enter our life, He will make possible a fullness that we alone will not be able to attain. If you truly love someone, you cannot desire anything less than this fulfillment.

The great message of *Amoris laetitia* is the announcement that the gladness that Jesus brings into the world can also penetrate the innermost depths of such an important reality in the life of a person as love, which becomes a stable relationship in marriage.

Regarding the discussion that followed the publication of the document about the possibility of granting the sacraments to people in a second union, in some cases and after an itinerary of discernment, I am reminded of Giussani's striking words at the November 1967 Student Youth Spiritual Exercises in Switzerland, about confession and participation in the Eucharist. I'll quote a significant passage:

> *You are inexcusable if you do not go to Confession. Inexcusable, because what keeps you from Confession is not what you have done, or the state of your soul ... First of all, it is the betrayal of yourselves, not of Jesus Christ or God, according to the understanding of the tradition in which you were educated. Even before, it is God and Christ, God and His revelation, inscribed in your humanity, in your flesh, it is the "more" that you deny. It is the lie against yourselves, the sin against the truth. This is the root of it all. This keeps you far from Confession: not desiring the good, not accepting to ask for good, only this. Not the fact that you foresee, saving a miracle, that tomorrow you will sin again, because the miracle can happen and you must ask for it if you want the good, if you want the "more," if you want to be true. The miracle can happen in twenty years, when the concubine dies. It does not matter, I say. I am not saying this to endorse a line of systematic adultery. I am saying this to centre on, to focus on the question in his heart, in his ultimate truth, in his essence. You are far from Communion not because of the state of your soul or because you do not feel you can go – and so you say it would be hypocritical. You are hypocrites, but not because it would be hypocrisy. You are hypocrites because hypocrisy is saying no to what is in us, maybe timidly because you are intimidated, full of fear because you are fearful, all foggy and vague because what is in us has not been nourished and educated by the social life in which we live, but even so it exists. It is because you say no to this "more," you crush this*

"more" underfoot, you continually inhibit the best of yourselves,
you do not desire the good, and for this reason you are far from
Communion. You are hypocrites when you say, "I am far
because it would be hypocrisy." Because receiving Communion
is a cry, the cry of a poor person, the cry of a derelict who no
longer understands or feels anything, and therefore turns to
force, to the Mystery, to the power that makes everything and
who will convert him; he turns to that mystery of God become
man who enters into his life, who reaches him with words and
facts with the mystery of the Church and tells him, "I am here,"
and who has changed many people and therefore will be able to
change you. A judgment and a desire for good, a cry to the
good: this is Communion. It is not a mood, a sentiment, a plea-
sure, or a merchant's sincerity.[22]

This is part of the proposal that Fr Giussani always made to
us: for him, the sacrament, Confession, the Eucharist, are the
simplest form of prayer, one that does not depend on your
mood. The Christian who stands in line to receive Communion may feel sad, discouraged, or confused, but simply by
being there, by approaching the altar to receive Communion,
he walks like a beggar, cries out, asks Christ to help him. For
this reason, Fr Giussani says that the greatest betrayal is
against your own desire, which dwells in the heart notwithstanding all kinds of situations and conditions. In fact, even
when a man has argued with his wife, and when he treats her
the opposite way than he had intended to, and feels inadequate, he nonetheless desires to love her. It is with this desire
of good that one goes to receive the sacrament, with this
recognition, even implicit. "Look, without You, Christ, I cannot manage. I come here limping, like a beggar asking You to
help me." The sacrament is not for the healthy. It is a help for
the sick. Christ valorizes even a small, minimum openness in
a person, bringing it to fulfillment. He tells us, "If you leave a
crack, a chink, I can enter, and I can do what you are unable
to do." This is what keeps this desire alive.

When you look at yourself only from the point of view of your capacity, at a certain point you get discouraged and end up saying, "This goal is not for me. It demands too much of me." But this is the crime. It is like giving up on the desire that notwithstanding all your sins still dwells within. This is the desire that Jesus valorizes. We see it in the Gospels. Why did He enter the home of Zacchaeus, a publican, who was trapped in a system of corruption?

Zacchaeus did not seem repentant when he climbed the tree and met the gaze of Jesus, who loved him first, called him first, embraced him first, and told him that he was coming to eat at his house. Zacchaeus just appears curious to us, not in the grip of an existential crisis of repentance for his sins.

Let's also think about how Jesus approached the adulteress who was to be stoned or the woman who washed His feet with her tears, or the Samaritan woman. What did Jesus valorize in them? He saw beyond the limitations, mistakes, and sins they committed; it is as if He did not let Himself be fooled, distracted, conditioned by all the evil. Under all the detritus of evil and sin, Jesus recognized the ineradicable presence of a desire for good, for fulfillment, and affirmed it. When those people found themselves looked upon in this way, embraced, and loved, their desire was reawakened in all its capacity. "Give me this water you speak of," said the Samaritan woman. Zacchaeus joyfully received Jesus in his home. The adulteress was shocked by the tenderness of Jesus, who did not condemn her. The sinful woman heard Him say that she had been forgiven a great deal because she had loved greatly. Being looked at and embraced with this mercy throws your heart wide open and reawakens hope. Trapped in similar situations, any one of us feels born again if we receive a similar gaze, a gaze that frees us, an embrace that precedes us, a love that takes the first step toward us. Christ *primerea*, Pope Francis says. Is this then a justification for our sins? No. Rather, it is the greatest challenge that a man and a woman can have to the prison of their sins. The outcome of being embraced is an other.

In this regard, I have always been struck by this passage from
Fr Giussani's book *The Attraction of Jesus*: "You can perfectly
well cry out for fifty years to God to enable you to overcome a
defect, seriously, and for fifty years you can always sin." But "we
should never be afraid, should never become discouraged
about anything," should never fall into moralism, but rather,
we should entrust ourselves ever anew to the One who has the
power to change our lives. "The time and the outcome are not
ours, and the power of God is greater than all our weakness. In
any case, even when we err, we are serene and glad. If you err
and you are not glad, you err there, because you show that you
trusted in yourself. Instead, no. You should entrust yourself to
Jesus. The Lord, who came to save you, knows how to save you!
Therefore, even if you err today, and err tomorrow, and err the
day after tomorrow, you are sure that the One who called you,
"the One who began this good work in you will bring it to
completion," will fulfill your desire to change, your desire to
overcome sin. "But you are not the one to decide the times. To
my mind, this is the most important question of the spiritual
life, of ascesis: the relationship with Jesus is the one phenomenon in which there is no mathematics, no quantity."[23]

Because of his experience of faith, this is the way Giussani
looked at the human journey and our historical situation. This
has always been the nature of the Church's companionship in
my life. Therefore in *Amoris laetitia* the pope insists on the
need to accompany people with the same gaze of mercy that
we receive, without getting discouraged by those who err, continuing to be open to the infinite mercy for which we are des-
tined, thanks be to God. As the Church teaches, and as happened for the good thief, the possibility of salvation, of
reaching Paradise, exists up to the very end, even in the last
moment of life. Up to the last moment, I can open myself to
the mercy of Christ, and this attitude decides my life. Fr Giussani taught us that this should be our attitude in every
moment, as if each moment were our last. I may have sinned
five minutes ago, but now, if I acknowledge Christ and place
myself before Him like the good thief, this enables me to start

anew. The other attitude, that of relying on yourself, makes you discouraged and burdened and in the end you give up.

The great challenge of the Church faced with the complex situation of many families today is to accompany people, to reawaken and stimulate the desire for fulfillment that dwells deep in their hearts, the openness to the infinite mercy that is Christ. The primary need is not for advice, but for places where this experience can happen. I have often observed this: couples who co-habitated but did not want to marry because of the troubled experiences of their parents or the negative stories of their friends were reborn when they found along their journey families who lived life with fullness. Over time, without anyone saying anything to them, they decided to get married, not out of moralism or to obey a rule, not because they "had to" get settled, but because they did not want to miss the beauty of a life that they saw reverberating in the families they had encountered. When they can see and experience the newness that comes into family life where the Christian faith is authentically lived, even people who never contemplated marrying, or who had a complicated situation, begin to want to take steps in that direction.

I'm struck by something you just said. In the dialogue with the pope about mercy, there was a point when, looking over the text, he wanted to correct where I had summarized his thought incorrectly. He explained that Jesus is there, waiting for us. God is there to give His mercy, and you just have to take a step. Actually, he also added, "Or at least desire to do it." You can be so closed, so limited, so bound up and immobilized in your sin and your limits that you are not even able to take a step. But the pope says that even just the desire to take that step, the realization that you live in a situation where you would like to take a step, even if you do not have the strength to do it, is already something. Even the desire is a crack where the grace of God can begin to enter and act.

Certainly, because desire is the greatest expression of the human person. Nothing expresses more succinctly our humanity than this desire. Fr Giussani identified morality with these two words: memory and desire. It is the desire constantly kindled by the presence of something beautiful. When you see something beautiful, even if you cannot live it yet, you cannot help but desire it. You may be incapable of living it, but you are unable to not desire it. The question is whether I follow my desire for the beauty I see, the good I sense, the fulfillment to which I aspire. Even if I am bumbling in my way of achieving it, even if a moment later I err again, it is as if my own desire does not give up in me: saying yes to this desire, following it, is the simplest form of prayer. The desire becomes prayer and prayer is nothing other than the ultimate expression of our desire to live up to the fullness for which we were created and to which we are called.

The Eucharist *"is not a prize for the perfect but a powerful medicine and nourishment for the weak,"*[24] *as the pope reminded us, quoting Saint Ambrose. What does this mean?*

The Eucharist is for us, for all of us, precisely because we are weak and need His grace moment by moment. The Eucharist is for people just as they are, fragile and sinful. The reduction of Christianity to ethics and moralism has prevailed to such an extent that we find it difficult to understand that the Eucharist is precisely for people like us, for the only kind of women and men who have ever existed in history, namely sinners who make mistakes, who fall, who need to get back up and need a hand of mercy that lifts them. Jesus's profound realism about the human condition and His profound passion for us gave Him the idea of the Eucharist. "Without Me you can do nothing,"[25] He warned us. In order to respond to this need, He wanted to remain present in His Church in this unique sacramental sign. With this awareness He told His disciples, "Amen, amen, I say to you, unless you eat the flesh of the Son of Man and drink His blood, you do not have life within you."[26] This is the strength that is communicated to us when we allow the power of Christ into our life, a strength that makes possible what nobody can achieve on his own. In fact, none of our human efforts succeed in achieving what our heart desires, the fullness to which it aspires.

The alternative is simple: since we cannot arrive by our own strength, we either give up and are convinced that it is impossible to find an answer to our desire for fullness and the skepticism that is so prevalent today takes over, or we open ourselves to another, we seek, ask, and – in the degree to which we have an encounter – accept He whose companionship enables life to attain the hoped-for fullness. The Eucharist is this Presence – the presence of Christ who remains in history – that becomes food, nourishment, support, regardless of our moods and mistakes. This Presence continues to be offered to each of us, poor wretches that we are, so that we can make a journey in life.

At times is there the risk of forgetting this primacy of grace that acts in us, and of believing instead that salvation is the fruit of our capacity, our goodness, our faithfulness and coherence?

The risk is enormous and continual, because in the common mentality the ideal is the human person who produces himself. The temptation of Prometheus is always at hand. The human person is so great, has such powerful aspiration, an ability to dream and to desire that is so beyond any measure that in a certain sense this temptation is unavoidable. But let's ask ourselves, is Prometheism the appropriate road for reaching the fullness that the human person desires? The Tower of Babel is an emblem of the outcome of the human attempt to build something to resolve the situation with our own energies.

In this sense, I think about the events of the last century, the various attempts to revolutionize history that failed and in many cases worsened the situation they sought to change. Many myths have collapsed. It is a dramatic and at times tragic human experience that concerns everyone. Not only have we experienced this temptation over and over, and verified its consequences, but we live it daily. We all know how easily we pass from the presumption of self-sufficiency and dominion over things, from the illusion of perfecting ourselves, to the most total discouragement, to the point of saying there is nothing to be done.

The Church, with her continual starting anew from the grace of Christ, with her openness to being suffused and filled by this operating grace, always enables people – even if they are sinners, and even if they do it limping – to get up again and walk. The Church enables us to get on track again and build, not according to Promethean pride, but with the new energy liberated by the grace of Christ.

I wanted to take the opportunity to clarify a point we have returned to often during our dialogue. I am referring to what is defined as the method of the movement, namely, the encounter, a reality that is encountered and that changes your life. In order to avoid misunderstanding, isn't it worth reiterating that this is never an automatic thing? When we speak of grace, it means that we are not talking about the consequence of a certain series of facts. Faced with testimony, one person may remain indifferent, while another may be struck. Thus the grace of God to call and convert hearts is unforeseeable and free. You cannot take for granted the outcome of the encounter with people who testify to the beauty of Christianity. Otherwise there is the risk of believing that it is sufficient to apply a method in order to obtain results.

I think this is a very beautiful observation. In fact, many times it is as if we believed in an evidence that has no need of the "I," no need of freedom. Once again, we can see this in experience. When someone falls in love, she is so swept away by what is happening that the prevalent sensation is of being fascinated and moved by the person who has burst into her life. She does not realize that actually she is adhering to and following a fascination and that her adherence to that attraction is not taken for granted. She could say no. There is never anything automatic in the human. The greatness of the "I" is in freedom. Even with all the fascination you can feel, with all the attraction you can experience, you can always say no. When you say yes, it is always through your freedom. At times, it is so simple to adhere, so simple to allow yourself to be swept away, that you do not realize that through your freedom you are following the fascination that the other person exerts on you. Then, when things get difficult and you have to consciously engage your freedom, you think it is different from the beginning. This brings a need to the surface: if we want the thing that fascinates us to become our own, if we want our adhesion to what attracts us to become certain, we have to put our freedom into action knowingly in every moment of the journey. Therefore Fr Giussani, speaking to students who were making the transition from high school to university and were called to live a more mature experience of what they had begun, said, "Expect a journey, not a miracle that gets you out of your responsibilities or neutralizes your struggle, making your freedom mechanical,"[27] making your freedom seem superfluous.

This journey is indispensable for true growth of my person, so that what I receive becomes mine. The episode I mentioned before comes to mind. During a lesson at the Università Cattolica [Catholic University] I talked about Fr Giussani, who in *The Religious Sense* invited readers to imagine being born with the awareness of an adult. He said that the first impression when faced with reality, with things, would be amazement. During the break, the student I mentioned came to the podium and told me, "It happened to me. I miraculously survived a car crash, and when I woke up from the coma, here too, as if miraculously, I looked at all of reality with a sense of wonder I'd never had before." Everything was new and fascinating; every encounter filled him with wonder. "But now," he added, "listening to you talk, I realized that the formalism has already returned again." I told him, "Look, don't expect everything from the miracle. You were given the miracle to wake you up, but this is the beginning of a journey, and if you do not make it, at a certain point you will find you are back to the way you were before." He had had a miracle, but it was not enough. He was already falling into automatism. He needed to accept making a journey, keeping alive the openness generated by that miracle with an education of freedom, so that his attitude of amazement when faced with reality would truly became his, without thinking that it was the product of a mechanism that excluded his freedom.

Often you hear it said that a Christian is free from the outcome. What does this mean? Do you agree?

Certainly. Not because the outcome is not desirable, but because the outcome that interests our humanity is already there. We already have it, given to us in the encounter with Christ. You can be free from the rest, without being indifferent. The outcome that most interests a child is not the one he obtains when he manages to do something well or when he has the best toys. It is the peace and joy that only the presence of his parents can give him. The relationship with them is what makes him live and enables him to grow, to correct himself when he makes mistakes, to be always curious, to learn. The Gospel helps us understand this with the story of the ten lepers. All ten received the grace of healing, but only one realized what had truly happened to him. In fact, all of them returned home happy and healed, except one, who returned and fell at Jesus's feet to thank Him. "He was a Samaritan. Jesus said in reply, 'Ten were cleansed, were they not? Where are the other nine? Has none but this foreigner returned to give thanks to God?' Then he said to him, 'Stand up and go; your faith has saved you.'"[28] The tenth leper understood that the most important thing was not the healing, but having encountered One who could bring his life to its authentic fulfillment.

I would like to tell you about my experience of this Gospel passage of the lepers. I was in the third year of middle school and I was searching. I felt a lack of satisfaction. For example, I looked forward to Saturdays to have fun, but something was missing for me. The expectation of Saturday was almost more beautiful than Saturday itself. I still remember as if it were yesterday the day I heard this passage at Mass in my parish. I was very struck because I realized that I was like the other nine lepers. I had received everything; I lived in a situation of goodness and positivity, with a family that loved me. All things considered, my life was carefree and glad, but I was unable to express any gratitude or acknowledgment. This really marked me. It was like my awareness passed from the adherence a child of that age can have, brought to Church by his parents, to the recognition of what I needed. I learned it from the one leper who returned to thank Jesus for being healed.

Starting from this experience, you see how simply going to Sunday Mass, maybe distracted some of the times, you expose yourself to being touched by Jesus's mantle. What a wonderful, horizon-opening thing for a kid! And even more so for adults, because they are more aware of their own limits. A kid can hope for satisfaction from his day off school, and many adults look for satisfaction from success at work, or money, power, or prestige. But there are moments of silence or calm when the confusion around us disappears and a sense of incompleteness emerges. Already as a young person, and then in any moment of life, you can be reached by a provocation like this. The important thing is not to succeed sometimes, but to succeed always – because each of us needs to be happy every day – and for the success be true.

Who can give this fullness? The answer is not in our hands. We do not have it. To help the kids understand, I used to say, "Let's suppose that what you did this weekend gave you real satisfaction. So the question is whether the whole week can become like this weekend." I proposed this example: "Imagine an overcast Tuesday in November, still a few days off from the weekend. Can something change on this Tuesday?" After a few moments of waiting for them to identify with the situation, I answered, "Yes, it can change, if, let's say, Monday evening something new happens. Imagine that on Monday you receive a long-desired 'yes' from the girl you're in love with. Tuesday, even though weekend is far off, even with all the weight of your studies, your life explodes." So the problem is for an event to enter into our life that can give every day the meaning of the weekend (used here as the symbol of an experience of authentic fullness). Otherwise we will always wait and postpone everything to a tomorrow that then will not satisfy us, no matter how "strong" the experiences we have, like travel to exotic countries, extreme sports, or now this terrible game of selfies in front of an oncoming train. A few years ago a

Ukrainian young man told me that what attracted him about the Christian experience he had encountered, even more than the great moments, was the change in daily life.

To summarize these reflections on the method and automatism, we can say that the journey – perhaps this is the most beautiful word to use – is a road upon which you are helped always to keep a wound open, always to keep your wounded heart open and tender. You are helped to keep your prayer of entreaty alive so that without any automatism you can be wonderstruck, can allow yourself to be called into question, can let your heart be fascinated and touched by the encounter with Christ today.

In effect, this was the great genius of Christ: He remains as a permanent companion in history. "I am with you always, until the end of the age."[29] He is with us in this sign that is the Church, limping and full of limits as it may be, full of mistakes and sins, yet it is the place where you are constantly put back on track, where you find the place to start fresh over and over again, so that you can continue walking tirelessly, shaky on your feet but always fighting. There is nothing more worth our while than a presence like that of the Church, a presence that incessantly reawakens us, that disentangles us from the oppressive workings of our own thoughts or moods, opens the door of the cage in which we have closed ourselves, to enable us to walk again, to enable us to begin once again the great adventure.

In the Church we can experience a Presence that embraces our life in all its incapacity, fragility, and weakness. I happen to meet sick people for whom things have gone differently than they had hoped, or people who have lost their job, and I am amazed to see how they start fresh from the awareness of this embrace. When something terrible happens in life, the difficult thing is to start over again. How can a person who has lost her job, maybe after having held prestigious positions, get over the blow and the humiliation? You need to receive the embrace of a presence that enables you to realize that life is not just success, and you need to accept it. Otherwise it will be difficult to start again. Friends who help people who have lost their jobs tell me that many of them need a companionship that restores them to themselves, that gives them back a true gaze upon themselves, so that the sense of failure will not dominate. When trouble of this kind happens, you can begin again from your own ashes, from your own sin, from your own mistake, from your own failure, from your own defeat, only through a Presence that measures up to the human drama. In His companionship you can always begin again, recognize and experience that life is bigger than our capacity for achievement, our capacity for success. There are people who give up and throw in the sponge. But we have seen people like Mother Teresa of Calcutta and John Paul II, for whom the progression of life and difficulties did not take away that striving, that continual movement on the journey. Life can be lived this way, up to the end.

Why do you think Pope Francis speaks so often of the Pelagian risk?

Because there is a constant temptation to think you are sufficient unto yourself, to depend on your own merits and ability to succeed. You need a foundation in life, and there are two options: either you base yourself on what you succeed in doing, or you base yourself on the relationship with an other. Pelagianism is the great temptation not to depend on the relationship with an other and to try to depend on yourself. This phenomenon appears over and over in history. We see it in the Gospel, in Phariseeism, which was the attempt to depend on your own works. We see it again promoted by the monk Pelagius – hence the name – in the times of Saint Augustine, as the attempt to place hope in the human person's capacity for moral coherence. In modernity it appears again in Immanuel Kant's reduction of Christianity to purely rational ethics. It is also present in many forms in today's mentality. From a certain point of view, it is a very human temptation, yet at the same time it is doomed to inevitable failure, as expressed in a vibrant and desperate way in the cry of the clergyman Brand in Ibsen's work, which Giussani read out resoundingly in Saint Peter's Square before John Paul II

in 1998: "Answer me, God, in the moment of death! If not by
Will, how can Man be redeemed?"[30] This is the drama. With
all our promethean efforts, with all the great drive we can
exert in our lives, in the end, desperation prevails.

In order to valorize the idea of merit, Christianity does not
entrust the human person's fulfillment to what we can do but
to the relationship with the presence of Christ, the foundation
upon whom Christians can ground their whole life. If a person's substance consists in her performance, how can she
avoid anger, displeasure, and disappointment? As Saint Francis
said to Brother Leone, who defined purity of heart as having
no faults to reproach, "I understand your sadness, since we
always have something to reproach."[31] The great alternative is
for the human person to consist in a relationship. Saint Paul
said this in a definitive way: either you rest on your works,
placing all your hope there, or your salvation depends on faith,
on the acknowledgment of a Presence.[32] In each of us, in our
way of looking at ourselves, in our way of looking at others
and at circumstances, either one or the other alternative prevails. With his whole Pharisaical tradition behind him, Paul
chose to rest on the foundation of Christ. The fact of Christ so
totally won him over that he had to rethink everything, and
the things he previously considered a gain he later deemed as
rubbish. The bond with the Risen Christ revolutionized his
way of conceiving of things, and his whole theology was a
rethinking of what he believed before in the light of the new
event that had happened to him. Otherwise, Christ would have
died in vain.[33]

The temptation of Pelagianism always lies in wait. The
Church, faced with any kind of desperation, faced with people
who find no peace, not even in the things they succeed in
doing, will always be present to tell them, "There is another
possibility, if you want; there is another possibility. If you allow
yourself to be embraced by an Other, there is another possibility. On your own, you end up like the pastor Brand in
Ibsen." Brand believed in the power of the will, treated everyone harshly, was an extremist in his attitudes, and ended up

dying alone with that cry to God. But the answer he obtained was "God is love!"[34]

Announcing the schedule for Francis's 25 March 2017 visit to Milan, Cardinal Angelo Scola explained that the pope's way of bearing witness to the faith draws in even those far away and people from other religions. "An openness that extends 360 degrees," he said, "a magisterium that passes to a great extent through acts and images, not only through words, as in contrast we Europeans, the heirs of intellectual and doctrinal visions, are accustomed."[35] How important are intellectualism and doctrinalism to us Europeans?

More than you would think. As Cardinal Scola noted, Pope Francis is the realization of the Second Vatican Council for our days, in the sense, as I have mentioned many times, of the council's affirmation that God's way of communicating Himself is not just through a set of doctrines, but through "deeds and words having an inner unity."[36] Francis communicates not only with words but also with actions. Through them both the simplest people and the intellectuals who are the furthest away are immediately reached and engaged by the newness contained in Christianity.

Christianity remains interesting for the people of our time only if it is proposed in its originality, as an event, a real presence that you can touch, hear, and see, as so beautifully expressed in the First Letter of John: "What was from the beginning, what we have heard, what we have seen with our eyes, what we looked upon and touched with our hands concerns the Word of life – for the life was made visible; we have seen it and testify to it and proclaim to you the eternal life that was with the Father and made visible to us."[37] The pope testifies about the nature of Christianity to the whole world. It seems to me a fact of great importance, a grace for which we must be grateful to God, one that contributes to free us from reductions that always lie in wait inside and outside the Church. As heirs of a certain history, we Europeans are easy prey to "intellectualistic and doctrinalistic visions," to use Scola's words. We have a cultural history with its directions, the fruit of a complex itinerary that we cannot get into here. I just want to stress that being continually freed from certain reductions is fundamental, precisely for understanding the doctrine. In fact, we are introduced to authentic comprehension always and only through lived experience. In this regard, Fr Giussani proposed a very effective observation: "Even a definition must reflect the experience of an acquisition. Otherwise, it would prove to be a schematic imposition."[38] Many times we have sought to communicate definitions instead of promoting the acquisition of their content of truth through experience. But this does not lead to any results, as we have observed in the relationship with many of our contemporaries.

Let's return to the origin. Jesus had to explain a new thing that could not be explained simply, because people would not have understood if it were only explained. First, it had to be lived as experience. Only in this way could the words acquire all their depth and breadth. When Jesus began His public life, He acted and spoke ("did and taught"). In order to show the meaning of what He said, He carried out gestures and He performed miracles: He healed the sick, forgave sinners, and looked at people with incomparable mercy and compassion. In the Synagogue, He spoke differently than the scribes and doctors of the law. Everyone was amazed, to the point of saying, "We have never seen anything of the kind!" Only this experience enabled people to comprehend the meaning of the words of Jesus. Without the actions that accompanied them, His words could have been reduced to the mentality of the time. Think of the word conversion. In the context of Phariseeism, conversion meant observing rules, and thus in the final analysis, a fiercer moralism. When Jesus said, "Convert!" how could they understand the meaning He gave to this word? He added, "Believe in the Kingdom of God."[39] What did it mean to believe in the Kingdom of God? He had to explain it not by explaining but by making it happen through His actions, the miracles, forgiving sins, preaching, speaking with authority, and His new way of looking at people and being in reality. This was the Kingdom of God. When He told His disciples, "Let's go to other cities, where I must announce the

Kingdom of God,"[40] this meant doing what He had done previously. The words explained the actions and the actions
helped them understand the words.

Without this, Christianity could not have entered into the
experience of the people, be grasped in its newness, and
spread to others; it would have been reduced to the usual measures, to the parameters of the culture of the time, because
there is no such thing as a world without culture. We all are
born into a given culture, history, and perception of reality. In
order to communicate itself in its newness, Christianity must
be able to throw wide open the measure of our mind, to generate greater openness in those who receive it. In other words,
it must be an event. Only in this way will it not be reduced to
the frameworks currently in fashion; only this way, as it says in
the Gospel, can new wine be put into new wineskins. With his
magisterium and testimony, Pope Francis reminds us of this:
we cannot put new wine into old wineskins. Christianity cannot be reduced to intellectualism or Pelagianism, to a system
of ethics or a series of practices, even if good ones.

That there is someone like the pope who communicates to
the world the original nature of the Christian fact is a great
and precious gift for everyone, none excluded.

Notes

PREFACE

1 L. Giussani, *Uomini senza patria (1982–1983)* (Milan: Biblioteca Universale Rizzoli, 2008), 96–7.
2 E. Mounier, *L'avventura Cristiana* (Florence: Libreria Editrice Fiorentina, 1951), 9.

CHAPTER ONE

1 C. Péguy, *The Portal of the Mystery of Hope*, trans. David Louis Schindler (Grand Rapids, MI: Eerdmans, 1996), 7.
2 C. Pavese, *Dialogues with Leucò*, trans. D.S. Carne-Ross (Venice: Marsilio, 1989), online edition.
3 E. Carrère, *The Kingdom*, trans. J. Lambert (London: Penguin, 2018), 144.
4 T.S. Eliot, "The Rock," *Collected Poems, 1909–1962* (New York: Harcourt Brace Jovanovich, 1991), 147.
5 Benedict XVI, *Christianity and the Crisis of Cultures*, trans. Brian MacNeil (San Francisco: Ignatius Press, 2006), 50–1.
6 I. Kant to F.H. Jacobi, 30 August 1789, *Philosophical Correspondence 1759–1799* (Chicago: University of Chicago Press, 1967), 158.
7 Ibid.
8 Benedict XVI, *Christianity and the Crisis of Cultures*, 51.

9 H. de Lubac, *The Drama of Atheist Humanism* (San Francisco: Ignatius Press, 1995), 70.

10 Ibid.

11 R. Guardini, *La fine dell'epoca moderna: Il potere*, 8th ed. (Brescia: Morcelliana,1993), 99.

12 Ibid.

13 J. Le Goff, "Perché l'Europa," posted 1 April 2014, Editori Laterza, www.laterza.it/index.php?option=com_content&view=article&i d=1377&Itemid=101.

14 G.B. Montini, "La distanza del mondo," *Azione Fucina*, 10 February 1929, 1; quoted in D. Agasso and A. Tornielli, *Paolo VI: Il santo della modernità* (San Paolo: Cinisello Balsamo, 2014).

15 C. Péguy, *Lui ⊞qui: Pagine scelte* ed. D. Rondoni, and F. Crescini, (Milan: Biblioteca Universale Rizzoli, 2009), 110.

16 Matthew 9:36.

17 Francis, general audience, St Peter's Square, Vatican City, 17 May 2017, http://w2.vatican.va/content/francesco/en/audiences/2017/ documents/papa-francesco_20170517_udienza-generale.html.

18 Augustine, "Sermo sancti Augustini cum pagani ingrederentur," in *The Works of Saint Augustine: A Translation for the 21st Century*, part 3, *Sermons*, vol. 11, *Newly Discovered Sermons*, ed. J.E. Rotelle, trans. E. Hill (Hyde Park, NY: New City Press, 1997), 379.

19 Cf. J.G. Lessing, "On the Proof of the Spirit and of Power," in *Lessing's Theological Writings: Selections in Translation*, trans. Henry Chadwick (Stanford, CA: Stanford University Press, 1957), 51–2.

20 T.S. Eliot, "The Rock," *Collected Poems, 1909–1962* (New York: Harcourt Brace Jovanovich, 1991), 164.

21 See Augustine, *De peccatorum meritis et remissione et de baptismo parvulorum*, [*A Treatise on the Merits and Forgiveness of Sins, and on the Baptism of Infants*] II, 19, 32.

22 Matthew 11:16–19.

23 Luke 14:1–6.

24 Mark 2:17.

25 Cf. John 6:35.

26 Cf. Mark 8:36.

27 Quoted in L. Smith, *Cesare Pavese and America: Life, Love and Literature* (Amherst: University of Massachusetts Press, 2008), 29.

28 C. Rebora, "Sacchi a terra per gli occhi," *Le poesie (1913–1957)* (Milan: Garzanti, 1988), 145.

29 Augustine, *The Confessions of Saint Augustine*, bk. 1, trans. F.J. Sheed (New York: Sheed and Ward, 1942), 3.

30 E. Montale, "L'agave su lo scoglio – Maestrale," *Ossi di seppia* (Milan: Mondadori 2003), verse 20.

31 C.S. Lewis, *Surprised by Joy: The Shape of My Early Life* (San Francisco: HarperOne, 2017), 268.

32 Benedict XVI, homily, Shrine of Aparecida, Brazil, 13 May, 2007, http://w2.vatican.va/content/benedict-xvi/en/homilies/2007/ documents/hf_ben-xvi_hom_20070513_conference-brazil.html.

33 Matthew 5:18.

34 Cf. Isaiah 58:12.

35 Francis, *Misericordia et misera* (apostolic letter), Rome, 20 November 2016, 1, http://w2.vatican.va/content/francesco/en/ apost_letters/documents/papa-francesco-lettera-ap_20161120 _misericordia-et-misera.html.

36 Luke 7:41–3.

CHAPTER TWO

1 G. Leopardi, *Pensieri*, vol. 68, trans. W.S. Di Piero (Emeryville, CA: Il Merlo Press, 2005), 113.

2 Luke 15:18–20.

3 Ibid.

4 Cf. A. Moravia, *Boredom* (New York: New York Review Books, 2004), 5.

5 R.M. Rilke, "The Second Elegy," *Duino Elegies*, trans. J.B. Leishman and S. Spender (New York: W.W. Norton, 1939), 31.

6 Cf. L. Giussani, *The Religious Sense*, trans. J. Zucchi (Montreal: McGill-Queen's University Press, 1997), 100.

7 A. Einstein, *Letters to Solovine*, trans. W. Baskin (New York: Philosophical Library, 1987), 132–3.

8 Cf. J.H. Newman, *Apologia pro vita sua* (Charleston, SC: BiblioBazaar, 2008), 40.

9 Genesis 1:4, 10, 12, 18, 21, 31.

10 Luke 22:42.

11 Matthew 27:46.

12 Luke 23:46.

13 John 14:31.

14 Cf. Luke 23:24.

15 Benedict XVI, Address at Auschwitz-Birkenau, Poland, 28 May 2006, http://w2.vatican.va/content/benedict-xvi/en/speeches/2006/may/documents/hf_ben-xvi_spe_20060528_auschwitz-birkenau.html.

16 Romans 8:35–9.

17 Benedict XVI, interview, *A Sua immagine: Domande su Gesù*, Channel 1, Italy, 22 April 2011.

18 Francis, remarks to sick children and their families, Chapel of the Domus Sanctae Marthae, The Vatican, 29 May 2015, http://w2.vatican.va/content/francesco/en/speeches/2015/may/documents/papa-francesco_20150529_bambini-malati-santa-marta.html.

19 P. Rossi, interview by P. Di Stefano published as "Odio i profeti di sventura," *Corriere della Sera*, 6 June 2011.

20 Luke 23:34.

21 *Catechism of the Catholic Church* (Vatican City: Libreria Editrice Vaticana, 2018), pt. 3, sec. 1, ch. 3, art. 1, point 1960.

22 Acts of the Apostles 9:4.

23 Benedict XVI, address to the bishops of Portugal, Fátima, 13 May 2010, http://w2.vatican.va/content/benedict-xvi/en/speeches/2010/may/documents/hf_ben-xvi_spe_20100513_vescovi-portogallo.html.

24 International Theological Commission, *In Search of a Universal Ethic: A New Look at the Natural Law* (2009), 8, http://www.vatican.va/roman_curia/congregations/cfaith/cti_documents/rc_con_cfaith_doc_20090520_legge-naturale_en.html.

25 H. Arendt, *Between Past and Future: Eight Exercises in Political Thought* (New York: Viking, 1961), 174.

26 *Dogmatic Constitution on Divine Revelation: Dei Verbum*, 2, http://www.vatican.va/archive/hist_councils/ii_vatican_council/documents/vat-ii_const_19651118_dei-verbum_en.html.

27 L. Giussani, "Corresponsabilità: Stralci dalla discussione con
   Luigi Giussani al Consiglio internazionale di Comunione e Liberazione, Agosto 1991," *Litterae communionis-CL* (November
   1991): 33.
28 John XXIII, speech at the opening of the Second Vatican Council, 11 October 1962, http://vatican2voice.org/91docs/opening
   _speech.htm.
29 Cf. Luke 15:11–32.
30 Cf. Matthew 21:31.
31 Cf. Matthew 21:31.
32 B. Marshall, *The World, The Flesh, and Father Smith* (New York:
   Bantam Books, 1947), 44.
33 Cf. Philippians 3:8–9.
34 Augustine, "Sermon 174,4.4," *Sermons on Selected Lessons of the
   New Testament*, vol. 2 (Oxford: J.H. Parker, 1845), 893.

CHAPTER THREE

1 "The Grace of Baptism," *Catechism of the Catholic Church* (Vatican City: Libreria Editrice Vaticana, 2018), pt. 2, sec. 2, ch. 1, art.
   1, 7, point 1272.
2 John 6:67.
3 *Dogmatic Constitution on Divine Revelation: Dei Verbum*,
   http://www.vatican.va/archive/hist_councils/ii_vatican
   _council/documents/vat-ii_const_19651118_dei-verbum
   _en.html, 12.
4 Mark 8:27.
5 Cf. Galatians 3:1–7; Galatians 1:6.
6 Cf. Galatians 1:8.
7 Cf. John 10:37–8.
8 Luke 1:1–4.
9 The Fraternity of Communion and Liberation is a universal
   association of the faithful generated by the charism of Fr Luigi
   Giussani, approved and established as a juridical person by the
   Holy See on 11 February 1982. Its goal is the education to faith
   of the person and Christian testimony in the world; it seeks to
   foster and promote the engagement of the person with the

Christian experience, according to the magisterium and tradition of the Catholic Church, so that each person over time may
realize her or his own identity and vocation. This engagement is
actuated and supported in a lived communion, as a dimension
and fundamental need of the person, which makes the memory
of the event of Christ a daily experience, transfiguring existence
to the point of impacting all of society in appropriate times and
ways. Under the leadership of the pope and bishops, the members of the Fraternity participate in the life of the Church in
their respective dioceses and collaborate in Christian testimony
in every sphere – school and university, factories and offices, the
world of culture, neighbourhoods, and cities – and with work,
which is the specific form of the adult relationship with reality.

10 Cf. A. Savorana, *The Life of Luigi Giussani*, trans. C. Bacich and M.
Sullivan (Montreal: McGill-Queen's University Press, 2018), 1117.

CHAPTER FOUR

1 Cf. 1 Corinthians 1:27.

2 Cf. A. Savorana, *The Life of Luigi Giussani*, trans. C. Bacich and
M. Sullivan (Montreal: McGill-Queen's University Press, 2018),
133ff.

3 L. Giussani, *The Risk of Education: Discovering Our Ultimate
Destiny* (Montreal: McGill-Queen's University Press 2018),
xxxi.

4 Cf. M. Busani, *Gioventù Studentesca: Storia di un movimento cat-
tolico dalla ricostruzione alla contestazione* (Rome: Studium,
2016).

5 See T.S. Eliot, "The Rock," *Collected Poems, 1909–1962* (New
York: Harcourt Brace Jovanovich, 1991), I, 14: "Where is the Life
we have lost in living?"

6 J. Ratzinger qtd. in Savorana, *Life of Luigi Giussani*, 1169.

7 L. Giussani, *Un avvenimento di vita, cioè una storia: Itinerario di
quindici anni concepiti e vissuti* (Rome: Il Sabato, 1993), 44.

8 L. Giussani, S. Alberto, and J. Prades, *Generating Traces in the History of the World: New Traces of the Christian Experience* (Montreal: McGill-Queen's University Press, 2010), 117.

9 Cf. Acts of the Apostles 4:13.

10 Cf. L. Giussani, *Dall'utopia alla presenza (1975–1978)* (Milan: Biblioteca universale Rizzoli, 2006), 330.

11 L. Giussani, *Dalla liturgia vissuta: Una testimonianza* (San Paolo: Cinisello Balsamo, 2016), 27.

12 R. Guardini, *L'essenza del cristianesimo* (Brescia: Morcelliana, 1980), 12.

13 1 Thessalonians 5:10.

14 Cf. L. Giussani, *Il movimento di Comunione e Liberazione (1954–1986): Conversazioni con Robi Ronza* (Milan: Biblioteca universale Rizzoli, 2014), 109–10.

15 L. Giussani, interview by J. Dembinski published as "Monsignore, mi spieghi un po' CL," *30Giorni*, n. 4, (1988), 67.

16 G. Napolitano, "Portate, nel tempo dell'incertezza, il vostro anelito di certezza," in *Una certezza per l'esistenza*, ed. E. Belloni and A. Savorana (Milan: Biblioteca universale Rizzoli, 2011), 39.

17 S. Mattarella, "La Repubblica ha 70 anni: XXXVII Meeting per l'amicizia fra I popoli: Tu sei un bene per me," posted 19 August 2016, www.meetingrimini.org.

18 Giussani, *Il movimento di Comunione e Liberazione*, 155.

19 J. Ratzinger, *Truth and Tolerance: Christian Belief and World Religions* (San Francisco: Ignatius Press, 2004), 117.

20 Congregation for the Doctrine of the Faith, "Doctrinal note on some questions regarding the participation of Catholics in political life," sec. 2, point 3, http://www.vatican.va/roman_curia /congregations/cfaith/documents/rc_con_cfaith_doc_20021124 _politica_en.html.

21 L. Giussani, "The Long March to Maturity," *Traces* (March 2008), 1, point 2b.

22 Giussani, *Dall'utopia alla presenza*, 52.

23 Romans 7:18–24.

24 Francis, address to the Community of Christian Life (CVX) Missionary Students' League of Italy, 30 April 2015, http://w2.vatican .va/content/francesco/en/speeches/2015/april/documents/papa-francesco_20150430_comunita-vita-cristiana.html.

25 Ibid.

26 J. Carrón, "Da chi ha sbagliato un'umiliazione per CL," *La Repubblica*, 1 May 2012.

27 1 Thessalonians 5:10.

28 Francis, address to participants at the International Pastoral Congress on the World's Big Cities, Vatican City, 27 November 2014.

29 Cf. Declaration on religious freedom *Dignitatis Humanae*, December 1975, Preface, 1, http://www.vatican.va/archive/hist _councils/ii_vatican_council/documents/vat-ii_decl_19651207 _dignitatis-humanae_en.html.

30 Giussani, *Il movimento di Communione e Liberazione*, 25.

31 Benedict XVI in A. Metalli, "Quando Ortega disse a Bergoglio: 'Oggi pomeriggio sarai Papa,' *La Stampa*, 27 March 2015.

32 H.U. von Balthasar, *Theo-logic: Truth of the World* (San Francisco: Ignatius Press, 2000).

33 Benedict XVI, address to the German bishops, Cologne, 21 August 2005, http://w2.vatican.va/content/benedict-xvi/en/speeches /2005/august/documents/hf_ben-xvi_spe_20050821_german-bishops.html.

34 John XXIII, address on the opening of the Second Vatican Council, 11 October 1962, http://w2.vatican.va/content/john-xxiii/it/speeches/1962/documents/hf_j-xxiii_spe_19621011 _opening-council.html.

35 J. Ratzinger qtd. in Savorana, *Life of Luigi Giussani*, 1168.

36 L. Giussani qtd. in ibid., 316.

37 L. Giussani qtd. in ibid., 314.

38 John Paul II qtd. in L. Giussani and G. Feliciani, *The Fraternity of Communion and Liberation: The Work of the Movement* (Milan: Società Cooperativa Editoriale Nuovo Mondo, 2005), 6.

39 J. Ratzinger, "Presentazione del nuovo Catechismo," *L'Osservatore Romano*, 20 January 1993.

40 Giussani, *Un avvenimento di vita*, 76.

41 *Dogmatic Constitution on Divine Revelation: Dei Verbum*, 8, http://www.vatican.va/archive/hist_councils/ii_vatican_council/d ocuments/vat-ii_const_19651118_dei-verbum_en.html.

42 John 16:13.

43 Cf. J.H. Newman, *An Essay on the Development of Christian Doctrine* (London: Aeterna Press, 2015).

CHAPTER FIVE

1 L. Giussani qtd. in A. Savorana, *The Life of Luigi Giussani*, trans.
    C. Bacich and M. Sullivan (Montreal: McGill-Queen's University
    Press, 2018), 578.
    John Paul II, "Go into the Whole World," Aula Paolo VI, 29 Sep-
    tember 1984, http://english.clonline.org/default.asp?id
    =562&id_n=14561.

3 L. Giussani qtd. in Savorana, *Life of Luigi Giussani*, 656.

4 John Paul II, prayer vigil with university student members of
    the Communion and Liberation movement, Sala Regia, 26 Jan-
    uary 1980, http://w2.vatican.va/content/john-paul-ii/es/speeches
    /1980/january/documents/hf_jp-ii_spe_19800126_cl.html.

5 C.M. Martini qtd. in Savorana, *Life of Luigi Giussani*, 853.

6 C.M. Martini in C. Vaghi, "La carità è," *Litterae communionis-CL*,
    n. 3 (1990), 30.

7 L. Giussani qtd. in Savorana, *Life of Luigi Giussani*, 674–5.

8 Benedict XVI, address to the participants in the general assem-
    bly of the Priestly Fraternity of Saint Charles Borromeo, Vatican
    City, 6 February 2013, http://w2.vatican.va/content/benedict-xvi
    /en/speeches/2013/february/documents/hf_ben-xvi_spe_20130206
    _san-carlo.html.

9 J. Carrón, letter to the editor, *Corriere della Sera*, 4 September
    2012, translated as "In His Heart, There Was Always Room for
    Us," http://english.clonline.org/default.asp?id=559&id_n=19773.

10 C.M. Martini, *Alzati, va a Ninive* (Milan: Centro Ambrosiano,
    1991), 12.

11 Martini, *Alzati*, 9.

12 Francis, "Angelus," St Peter's Square, Vatican City, 26 March
    2017.

13 L. Giussani, *Il senso di Dio e l'uomo moderno* (Milan: Biblioteca
    universale Rizzoli, 2010), 126.

14 L. Giussani, *Porta la speranza*, (Genoa: Marietti 1820, 1997), 119.

15 Francis, Apostolic exhortation *Evangelii gaudium*, 1,
    http://w2.vatican.va/content/francesco/en/apost_exhortations/doc
    uments/papa-francesco_esortazione-ap_20131124_evangelii-
    gaudium.html.

16 Ibid., 7.
17 Ibid., 35, 11.
18 Ibid., 12.
19 Paul VI, Apostolic exhortation *Evangelii nuntiandi*, 41, http://w2.vatican.va/content/paul-vi/en/apost_exhortations /documents/hf_p-vi_exh_19751208_evangelii-nuntiandi.html.
20 Cf. Mark 6:34.
21 Cf. Matthew 19:10.
22 L. Giussani, *La familiarità con Cristo* (San Paolo: Cinisello Balsamo, 2008), 188–90.
23 L. Giussani, *L'attrativa Gesù* (Milan: Biblioteca universale Rizzoli, 2001), 267.
24 Francis, Apostolic exhortation *Evangelii gaudium*, 47.
25 John 15:5.
26 John 6:53.
27 L. Giussani qtd. in Savorana, *Life of Luigi Giussani*, 634.
28 Luke 17:16–19.
29 Matthew 28:20.
30 H. Ibsen, "Brand," *Plays 5: Henrik Ibsen: Brand, Emperor, and Galilean* (London: Methuen, 1986), 112.
31 É. Leclerc, *La sapienza di un povero* (Milan: Edizioni biblioteca francescana, 2012), 105.
32 Cf. Romans 3:21–31.
33 Cf. Galatians 2:21.
34 Ibsen, "Brand," 112, n.
35 A. Scola qtd. in A. Tornielli, "Il papa a Milano tra periferia e carcere," *Vatican Insider*, 17 November 2016.
36 *Dogmatic Constitution on Divine Revelation: Dei Verbum*, 2.
37 1 John 1:1–3.
38 L. Giussani, *At the Origin of the Christian Claim* (Montreal: McGill-Queen's University Press, 1998), 61.
39 Cf. Mark 15.
40 Cf. Luke 4:43.